A TRADITIONAL GROCER:

T. D. Smith's of Lancaster 1858-1981

by Jayne Broome, Louise Collins, Claire Gibbs,
Helen Jane and Anne Olliver

Edited by Michael Winstanley

Centre for North-West Regional Studies
University of Lancaster
Occasional Paper No. 21

First edition, 1991

General Editor: Oliver M. Westall

This volume is the twenty-first in a series published by the Centre for North-West Regional Studies at the University of Lancaster. Details of other titles in the series which are available may be found at the back of this volume.

ISSN 0308-4310

Published by the Centre for North-West Regional Studies, University of Lancaster.

Typeset in 10/11 Times Medium by Carnegie Publishing Ltd., Maynard St., Preston. Printed by T. Snape & Co. Ltd., Preston.

British Library Cataloguing in Publication Data
A Traditional Grocer: T. D. Smith's of Lancaster 1858–1981 – (Occasional Papers, Centre for North-West Regional Studies, 0308–4310, 21)
    1. Lancashire (England), history, 1858–1981.
    I. Winstanley, Michael.   II. Westall, Oliver M.
    III. University of Lancaster. *Centre for North-West Regional Studies.*   IV. Series:
    942.708092

ISBN 0-901272-89-2

Contents

Acknowledgements

We would like to take this opportunity to thank the many people who have aided us in this project. We are indebted to Michael Winstanley for all his help and encouragement without which we would not have reached the stage of being able to consider publication of this study. Our thanks go to Oliver Westall for his interest and guidance, and also the staff at Lancaster University Library, particularly Jennifer Bentley, John Illingworth and Ken Harrison. We must not forget Dave Bleasdale whose patience has been most admirable throughout the long haul of teaching us the intricacies of the word processor, and Ethel Gaddes and staff at Lancaster City Library for their help.

We owe a great debt to Ian Smith and his family for allowing us to consult the family scrapbook and for providing us with many photographs and additional information. Other grateful thanks go to Herbert and Annie Pyke, Tommy Seddon, Jim Redmayne, Norman Bradley, Leslie Jones and Edward Towers, whose personal memories have been of great value. Special thanks must go to Anne Pyke for typing out T. D. Smith's original manuscript autobiography and to Mr Edwards for the loan of an apprenticeship indenture from 1894. Unfortunately we were not able to visit everyone who offered us assistance in our project following an article in the *Lancaster Guardian*, but we would like to take this opportunity to thank them for their interest. We are grateful to our families and friends for their support, and would also like to thank one another for the pleasure and satisfaction we have gained from working together.

Jayne Broome
Louise Collins
Claire Gibbs
Helen Jane
Anne Olliver

June 1990

The research for this booklet was carried out by a group of five students of Lancaster University History Department as part of their undergraduate scheme of study. They were also responsible for most of the initial draft and for the illustrations and diagrams. The introduction, chapter one and subsequent revision are the responsibility of their tutor.

We are all particularly indebted to E. H. Booth & Co. Ltd., Ian, Joseph and Felicity Smith and the History Department of Lancaster University for the generous financial assistance which has made publication possible.

Michael Winstanley
March 1991

Preface

THE history of business is usually thought of in terms of great innovators, captains of industry or giant corporations that have individually had a great impact on their times. But they were surrounded by many smaller, often family-owned, firms that were far more representative of business life. Our knowledge of such firms is limited. Many did not survive for long; few leave adequate records for a history to be written.

T. D. Smith's is an important exception. It lasted for over a century, and sufficient records remain to enable us to construct a fascinating story, blending family and business history. It provides an opportunity to understand grocery concerns in country towns throughout England.

For more than a century it formed an important part of the life of Lancaster. It was also one of the channels through which successive generations of Lancaster people could participate in the widening range of foods and other household commodities that formed such an important element in the improvement in living standards that took place in the hundred years after 1860. Many Lancaster people will enjoy an opportunity to recall what became a noted institution in the town. In its own way the individual enterprise of T. D. Smith and his successors was therefore of social and economic significance, and its history therefore valuable.

This book is also a product of enterprise. It has been written by a group of students from the University's History Department under Michael Winstanley's supervision. They undertook the project as part of a scheme designed to encourage students to relate academic work more closely to the world of business. They have fulfilled this objective with flair and initiative and it is a pleasure to share the outcome with a wider audience.

Oliver M. Westall

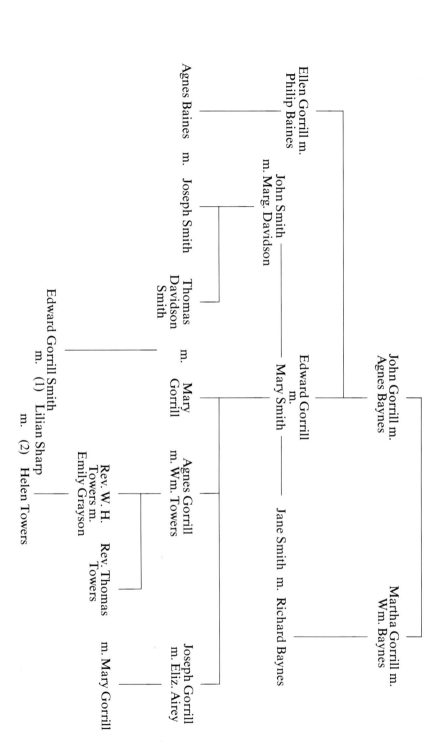

Figure 1: *Intermarriage in the farming community, c.1800–1940*

Introduction

T. D. SMITH, and shopkeepers like him, have been largely overlooked by historians. Studies of retailing have emphasised what they consider to be 'revolutionary' changes which have taken place over the last 150 years concentrating on co-operatives, multiples and departmental stores and on new forms of competition – especially the price cutting of branded products.[1] More recently there has been increased emphasis on the continued ability of small shopkeepers to survive well into the 20th century. The picture which tends to emerge from such studies, however, is of a polarised retail trade, dominated economically by a few large organisations, but numerically by a host of tiny family enterprises, often ephemeral, situated in suburban locations and with little scope for expansion.

Few have made more than a passing reference to the substantial, independent tradesmen, usually operating specialist businesses from centrally situated premises. Their decline has often appeared inevitable, ground between upper and nether millstones of price-conscious multiples and giant co-operatives on the one hand and, on the other, small neighbourhood shopkeepers relying on cheap or free family labour and the attractions of convenient hours and proximity to customers. The decline of the 'traditional' grocer in particular was widely forecast as early as the late-19th century in the trade press, by economic and social commentators and even by writers of popular fiction. 'In a few years time', declared Charles Booth in his study of London life and labour in the 1890s, 'the [grocery] trade will probably be confined to large firms and a certain number of very small shops in poor districts where the master is on the same social level as his customers'.[2] *The Times*, in a leader of 1902, confidently predicted the imminent 'Passing of the Grocer'.[3]

Yet it is only since the Second World War, and during the 1960s in particular, that the decline has been evident. Prior to that retailing was dominated by a numerous class of substantial businesses whose proprietors were often socially and politically prominent in their local environment. Lancaster's town centre, for example, was dominated by such traders until comparatively recently and even now (1990) a number of them who can trace their origins back over several generations remain in business: Whittakers' furniture stores, Atkinson's tea and coffee shop, Barrow's the tailors, Chirnsides' fashion shop and Gorrills' china and fabric business to name but a few. E. H. Booths, 'Grocers and Italian Warehousemen', have not only survived but have expanded operations from their Preston base all over the North West of England.[4] The independent, medium-sized family retailer has proved remarkably resilient.

Despite this, little is known about such businesses and the people who ran them. Reasons for this neglect are not difficult to find. To some extent it has simply reflected the cinderella image which retailing has suffered alongside the multi-nationals and large-scale producers which have been much more appealing to economic historians. Paucity of sources, however, has also presented a major problem. Many smaller transient shopkeepers simply kept no records, but the survival rate even among the established specialist retailers has also been very low. Historians who have sought to study them, therefore, have been forced back on to trade directories, themselves of dubious reliability, bankruptcy records of acknowledged untypicality, and on a trade press which consistently presented a public campaigning image and publicised 'best' as opposed to 'normal' practice.

This study of T. D. Smith's longstanding, successful grocery business is, therefore, uniquely valuable. From small beginnings as the proprietor of a single grocery shop in Penny Street, Lancaster, in 1858, Smith went on to build up an extensive network of branches in the town and an impressive delivery service extending throughout North Lancashire and into the West Riding of Yorkshire. After his death in 1906 the business was continued first by his son, Edward Gorrill Smith (assisted by his younger brother, Charles), and then by his grandson, Francis Brian Smith, before being passed on in 1961 to some of the senior staff who ran it until it finally closed in 1981. There are unusually rich sources covering both the business and the family: takings books for 1877-1903 and 1957-61,

staff wages books from 1904, miscellaneous adverts, posters, catalogues and samples, a family tree, a scrapbook of press cuttings, photographs, the memories of the family, employees and customers and, above all, an unpublished autobiography of the original proprietor written between 1902 and 1905. This manuscript, which was only discovered in the attic of the premises of the last shop on Dalton Square when it closed in 1981, proved to be an invaluable source of information, providing the basis of much of the early chapters. All unattributed quotations in this study are drawn from it. These sources not only enable us to draw a detailed picture of the shop itself, but give a rare insight into the values, mentality and place in local society of the middle-class, independent businessman.

This booklet explains how the family business adapted so well to the changing retailing scene without losing its essentially traditional image, and how the family fitted into provincial society. To begin with, however, it is necessary to appreciate something about the rural background of the original proprietor, Thomas Davidson Smith (1838-1906), who was responsible for building up the business and establishing its pattern of trade in the later nineteenth century.

Notes

1. See, for example, J. B. Jeffreys, *Retail Trading in Britain, 1850–1950* (1954), which emphasises the development of multiples; D. Alexander, *Retailing in England in the Industrial Revolution* (1970); W. H. Fraser, *The Coming of the Mass Market, 1850–1914* (1981). For a review of recent literature and oral recollections, see M. J. Winstanley, *The Shopkeeper's World, 1830–1914* (1983).

2. Charles Booth, *Life and Labour of the People of London*, vol. vii, (1896), p.220.

3. *The Times*, 18–20 August 1902.

4. *E. H. Booth & Company Ltd., 1847–1985*, (E. H. Booth, Manchester, 1985).

1

Family background

THOMAS Davidson Smith (hereafter abbreviated to T. D.) hailed from 'old yeoman stock' in the township of Tatham in the Pennine foothills some ten miles east of Lancaster up the Lune Valley.[1] The family's connection with Gamblesholme, a farmstead on the River Hindburn just to the east of the neighbouring village of Wray, can be traced back continuously to the sixteenth century. By the mid-19th century they had acquired other lands, most notably the adjoining farm of Mealbank, as well as a variety of small holdings and cottages in the area.[2] Despite the dispersal of some of these after the death of T. D.'s great uncle William Smith in 1838, their holdings remained significant. The tithe award for Tatham in 1848 shows T. D.'s uncle, Francis Smith, owning and occupying the 69 acres which comprised the Gamblesholme estate, and his father, John, in possession of the 71-acre Mealbank Farm which he had occupied since 1842. In addition, Francis owned several cottages in Wray which he rented out. But the family's interests extended beyond the ownership of land. Like Thomas Davidson of Summersgill Farm in Wray with Botton, T. D.'s maternal grandfather after whom he was named, the Smiths were 'esteemed as owners on a small scale, but farmers on a much larger scale'. Both Francis and John also rented land adjacent to their properties, Francis virtually doubling his acreage by this means. Before coming into his inheritance, John had also rented hill farms at Upper Thrushgill and Overhouses, adjacent to Summersgill, the former passing to Joseph,

his younger brother, who is shown as occupier there on the township tithe awards for 1849.[3] Their father, T. D.'s grandfather, also Joseph, had spent his life renting farms on short leases as far afield as Colne, Bentham, Ingleton, Yarlsber and Raygill before finally settling at Overhouses where his grandson was born on 10th October 1838.

The Smiths, then, were prominent local landowners and farmers whose agricultural activities were spread over a wide area. Farming, however, was a precarious existence, even for such men. T. D. stresses in his autobiography that, in the early-19th century in particular, many farmers were 'poor, ill fed and badly clothed' having to go to market in carts, 'eligible conveyances being a luxury which they could not at that time aspire to'. Surviving wills also indicate that many of the Smiths' more recent purchases were mortgaged, while Mary Smith, T. D.'s aunt, in her episodic diary, dwells on the physical disabilities, illnesses and premature deaths which the lifestyle entailed. But T. D. nevertheless came from a relatively prosperous background for the time, his uncle Francis being of sufficient status to occupy several positions of influence in the area, including the chairmanship of the Caton Gilbert Poor Law Union.[4]

The family's position in local society was consolidated through a complex series of intermarriages with other families of similar social standing over a geographical area which stretched from Lancaster in the west well into Yorkshire in the east. The extent of this was undoubtedly far greater than

Plate 1: *Mary Gorrill prior to her marriage to her cousin T. D. Smith in 1862.*

any single family tree can display. Even the household servant sent to summon the doctor from Bentham to attend on T. D.'s birth, for example, was a 'distant cousin' of his employer, John Smith.[5] Selected illustrations, however, can provide some understanding of the nature and significance of this extended family network.

In 1862 T. D. himself married his cousin, Mary Gorrill, daughter of his aunt Mary Smith (who kept the diary referred to above) and Edward Gorrill, son of John Gorrill, a prominent farmer in the region. Another of his aunts, Jane, married Richard Baynes whose family had intermarried with the Gorrills for at least three generations. Through the marriage of another of his cousins, Agnes Gorrill (his wife's sister), T. D. also became linked with

another prominent local farming family, the Towers of Stubb Hall, Halton, near Lancaster (see figure 1, page 6).

Such relationships were not only the warp and weft of the fabric of the farming community, linking families together in a mutually supportive, extended social network, they had implications for those like T. D. who left to start businesses in Lancaster, or further afield. His cousins, Joseph and John Gorrill, who were also his brothers-in-law, both set up in trade in the town, the latter as a shoe manufacturer with twenty outlets in the area, but with his main premises and living accommodation next door to T. D.'s grocery shop in Penny Street, and internally 'joined to and open to each other off a staircase'. William Glover Smith, T. D.'s brother, established himself as a draper and tailor and lived for much of his life in a house next door to T. D. on Regent Street, Lancaster. His nephew by marriage, R. G. Towers, nicknamed 'Towers of the Twenty Shops' by his family, also ran a chain of grocery stores in the late-19th century, while Helen Towers, daughter of another branch of the family, was later the second wife of T. D.'s son and business successor, Edward Gorrill (E. G.) Smith. After the First World War Mealbank Farm was let to yet another member of the Towers family.[6] Two of T. D.'s cousins, Joseph and William Baynes, emigrated to South Africa where they achieved considerable success and public prominence. Even at this distance, however, they were able to offer employment to Francis, another of T. D.'s sons, and hospitality to several of his spinster daughters and to E. G. Smith and his wife on a tour in 1911.[7]

The connections were reinforced by christening offspring with the forenames and surnames of earlier members of the family. All of T. D.'s children, for example, were named after forbears except the youngest, Charles Hermon, who took his middle name from the family's house on Regent Street, a decision later bitterly regretted by T. D. since William Baynes, 'said to be related in four or five different ways to my wife and myself', was visiting at the time; 'If we had given Charles his name . . . he might later have left him a considerable fortune. It was perhaps unwise of us, in this way, to manifest our usual independence.'

The Smiths' incorporation into the broader social community was strengthened by their Methodism. T. D.'s grandfather, Joseph, had established his farm at Overhouses as a meeting place and had collaborated with John Gorrill senior in promoting an active preaching circuit among the fell communities. His aunt Mary refers in her diary to memorable visits from prominent preachers, to religious celebrations at Davidson's neighbouring Summersgill Farm, and to visiting Lancaster for the opening of the Independent Methodist Chapel. T. D.'s father, John, offered hospitality at Mealbank Farm to itinerant preachers on the circuit and was actively involved in the building of the new chapel in Wray in 1848. His mother, despite being brought up as a 'church woman' who had sung in Tatham Chapel choir, had also attended the classes at Overhouses as a young woman and went on to become an indefatigable Methodist class leader and visitor for the rest of her life. Although relations were not always smooth, dissension leading to the formation of a breakaway sect in Wray in 1850 of which T. D.'s uncle Francis was a member, Methodism generally served further to integrate the scattered farming community. When, as a young grocer's apprentice in Lancaster in the 1850s, T. D. began to attend Sulyard Street Methodist Chapel on a regular basis, he was reaffirming what was already a strong connection with an established religious and social network which he, his brother William and his son Edward were to nurture for the rest of their lives.[8]

Family and religion also featured strongly in T. D.'s educational experiences. As in Cumbria, there was a long tradition of self-education in the upland Pennines, but this was clearly viewed as inadequate schooling for a career in business, or even

Plate 2: *Thomas Davidson Smith as a young man around 1860.*

farming. The local schools which supplemented this, and which T. D. first attended, offered little more it seems. His memories of the establishments at Tatham and Lower Salter, the latter at the head of the isolated Roeburndale valley where he boarded weekly with another uncle and aunt, Peter and Betty Skirrow, were far from flattering. They offered little beyond harsh, often unjust discipline, basic three Rs and rote learning of the Church of England catechism. In his early teens, his parents, 'desirous of giving me the best education which they could afford', sent him and his elder brother Joseph as boarders to a Leeds academy run by Richard Driver, yet another cousin of his father and an active Methodist class leader.

11

Here, for £30 a year, he learned 'plain commercial educational subjects', was 'well looked after in the writing and the formation of letters' and picked up 'some knowledge of measuration, land measure and a very little geometry', the last on the assumption that he, like most of his family, would continue in farming.

His decision to enter retailing was only taken on his return from Leeds when he began to suffer from 'sick, bilious headaches' while working in the fields in the summer. His anxious father gave the fourteen-year-old grudging support: 'If I pleased myself and did not succeed, I should have only myself to blame'. He was, in his own words, 'a country youth, possessed with strong aspirations, no little ambition, determination, enquiry and some natural talent for trading and acquisitiveness', but he was a country youth who also possessed several other important assets: his extended family, an intimate acquaintance with the Pennine Methodist farming community and a sound grounding in education and commerce. He was to draw on them all over the ensuing decades as he embarked on his grocery trade in Lancaster.

Notes

1. Obituary in *Lancaster Guardian*, 8 September 1906.
2. Information from last will and testament of William Smith, 13 July 1838, and family tree. Both in family possession.
3. Lancashire Record Office, Tithe Awards for Tatham (1848) and Wray with Botton (1849).
4. *Lancaster Guardian*, 8 September 1906; Mary Smith's diary is in the family's possession.
5. His name was John Dean. Significantly, Francis Smith rented out his cottages in Wray to an Elizabeth Dean.
6. Information drawn from Smith and Towers family trees, Census Enumerators' Schedules, Lancaster (1881), and an interview with Edward Towers, 16 May 1990.
7. Undated press cuttings in family scrapbook. E. G. Smith gave lectures to the town's grocers and assistants about his visit to South Africa on his return in 1911.
8. See chapter 5 and W. G. Smith's obituary, *Lancaster Guardian*, 29 April 1911.

2

The business: its origins and development

AS the only town of any size in North Lancashire, Lancaster had long functioned as a market centre for a wide rural hinterland. Its industrial base, however, was late in arriving, only really expanding from the 1870s as it specialised in linoleum and table baize and acquired a large railway waggon works which pushed up the population from 14,481 in 1861 to 40,320 forty years later, and led to the building of working-class suburbs on the outskirts, especially from the 1880s.[1] In the 1850s, however, there was little sign of this upturn in fortune, population even falling marginally during this decade. It did not, therefore, appear to be an auspicious place to set up in business when T. D. began his career in grocery as an apprentice to William Beckett of 42 Church Street Lancaster in April 1853, at the age of fourteen and a half years, remaining with him until his 19th birthday on 10th October 1857. In his autobiography he is fiercely critical both of the training he received and the business practices of his first employer, making clear that this was a 'lower class and medium farmers' business, who only bought the absolute requisites for a family'. He further complained that

> little opportunity was given for acquiring any technical knowledge of the quality of goods, to form a knowledge of the value of stock, or to be trained in the business modes, habits or the financial terms of various branches of the business.

T. D. clearly sought experience of a very different class of grocery. When his apprenticeship ended, therefore, he declined an offer to stay since he wished to improve himself and more especially his 'knowledge of goods of trade and general superior modes of business in good class shops'. With this in mind he obtained a situation with a wholesale firm of tea and coffee merchants, Meares and Richardson of Hanging Ditch, Manchester, and was sent to Messrs. Fernleigh and Co., Deansgate, Bolton, a retail firm in which Mr. Meares was the main financial partner. Despite the long hours, employment with this high-class 'tea, grocery and Italian business' was much more to his liking, the situation satisfying the young man's thirst for knowledge of his chosen trade:

> It was here that I took up and formed a knowledge of book keeping as part of my duties, also coffee roasting . . . there was a good staff of assistants [retail] and I got an insight into many details of high class business. At this and the previous place, I and all the other assistants lived on the premises, had long hours, 7.30am to 9.00pm Monday and Friday, 7.30pm other nights except Saturday, which was 11.30pm. There was always time to go in and dress for meals after shutting, but no more, not as now, with one hour for dinner and half an hour for tea, never outdoors for recreation except summer mornings before 7:30am. Time for private writing was Sunday. I stayed at this place until the end of October 1858, and got much valuable information. I had a wage of £26 after finding clothes, some in arrears. I was able to save half of it.

Just turned twenty years of age and with this training behind him, T. D. returned to

13

Plate 3: *A grocer's shop in Church Street, Lancaster, around the turn of the century, where T. D. Smith was first apprenticed in the 1850s. (From an old postcard, original in Lancaster City Museum.)*

Lancaster and commenced business on his own account on 12th November 1858, renting a small shop on the corner of Ffrances Passage and Penny Street, then the main shopping street in Lancaster, for £29 *per annum*. The premises were far from convenient, as a description in his auto-biography makes clear:

> It had a small cellar to the front but no convenience for the reception of goods, only a coal shute. All goods had to be carried in at the shop door. I had the greatest difficulty to lower the floor and widen the shop by taking out stone work to admit of fixtures and canisters.

Despite being 'full of energy, enterprise, enquiry and ambition', Smith apparently faced an uphill battle. He had but little capital to support his venture, in fact only £100 free of interest and £200 to £300 more

upon which he had to pay interest until he had saved sufficient to pay it off. His only assistance came from his sister Jane who acted as housekeeper and helped out in the shop, and one errand boy named Dowthwaite. Not only was Lancaster a depressed town but its retail trade was dominated by a few grocers who 'had the greatest part of the shop trade' by acting as wholesalers to smaller town grocers like T. D. as well as those who traded in the countryside immediately around Lancaster. Since these firms were 'especial monopolists for trading groceries' Smith's greatest difficulty lay in obtaining independent access to the best markets for buying essential articles of stock:

> I found myself with my small shop and capital, and trying to establish a new business, that I was farmed over, or

14

certain firms [H. R. Preston of Church Street and later Henry Welch] sought to monopolise over me, by preventing the representatives of the best London or Liverpool business houses from calling on me.

The growth of the business

T. D.'s response to these problems was to turn to the area he knew best, initiating the delivery service which was to remain a fundamental element in his success. Although he was by no means the only grocer in Lancaster to offer such a service, T. D. spotted a niche in the market, by dealing primarily with those 'farmers and other families' who lived outside an eight-mile radius of Lancaster, making particular use of his family connections in the hills to the east. He arranged to have his goods 'sent by rail and met at different stations and delivered by some farmer in the surrounding district free of charge to the purchaser'.

An extensive delivery network was rapidly established, mainly in the fells to the east, but also to the north in the villages around Carnforth and Grange over Sands. By 1878, when we have the first precise details of his trade, deliveries already accounted for £4,520 of his total turnover of £12,553, the majority of this (£3,074) being in the area from which he originated. Over the next twenty five years he further increased this trade to £7,089 (see figure 2).[2]

This growth, however, was by no means steady and was only achieved by extending his delivery network still further as income from his original areas stagnated. This was due to a combination of factors, most notably the depression which hit farming in the last two decades of the century and the fact that Grange was increasing in population and attracting substantial shops of its own, thereby ending the area's traditional dependence on Lancastrian firms for supplies. From the mid-1880s, therefore, he expanded southwards to just north of Garstang and then in the 1890s west to Pilling, while from 1892 he also

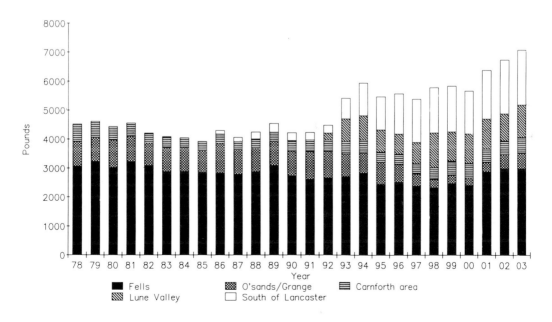

Figure 2: *The expansion of the delivery network and turnover, 1878–1903.*

concentrated more on the nearby villages of Slyne, Bare and Halton. Despite all this, however, Smith's dependence on deliveries between 1878 and 1903, the period for which we have detailed figures, declined from 36.1% to just 24.2% of turnover. The reasons for this lie in other aspects of the strategy he developed in the late-19th century.

Smith always placed great importance on the appearance of his main shop in Penny Street. In August 1867, as a result of the Preston bank failure, he was able to purchase the premises which he had previously been renting. Soon afterwards he extended into adjacent premises in Ffrances Passage by converting the cottage in which he had been living into another shop, linked internally but trading as a separate outlet. Further refurbishment was carried out after a fire in 1879-80,[3] but it was in the 1890s that the central premises were completely overhauled in an effort to compete with the emerging multiples such as Liptons, Home and Colonial and Slaters which were then appearing in the town:

It was deemed wise and desirable for the enlargement of the business, to have eligible accommodation for customers, and for cultivating a thoroughly high class and better middle class trade in the town and district.

Consequently Smith purchased the adjacent 17-19 Penny Street, which had previously belonged to the failed shoemaking firm of his cousin's widow, S. A. Gorrill and Son, for the sum of £4,400. These were then

altered, modernised and splendidly fit up, by new fronts, fixtures, decorated offices, warehouse, cellars, seweraged, ventilated, cemented and adapted for our business . . . at a cost of £1100 to £1200.

The original premises were rearranged, the frontage on Penny Street being 'fit up' and let as a separate shop while the Ffrances Passage shop was also improved. This refurbishment boosted trade at the central premises in the late-1890s from just £6,501 in 1895, to £9,807 five years later, much to T. D.'s satisfaction: 'The returns of the business, have increased and this with all the increased opposition . . . in the town'. In 1937 the central store was modernised again for the last time, retaining the same appearance and style until its closure in 1961.

But reliance on trade at the central stores was not enough. The improvements of 1896/7 merely restored turnover to the levels of twenty years earlier. For much of the intervening period trade at his town-centre shops had been in ominous decline, despite the increasing size and prosperity of the population. T. D. recognised that yet more was needed. The answer was a branch network.

During the early-1880s the firm had operated a business at Lord Street, Southport for six years but

after giving it a fair trial and with the great difficulty of getting suitable men to manage, and the town and working expenses so great and the great difficulty of bringing up a sufficient value of business, there being no manufacturing in the town and very little working class from whom to draw trade . . . we decided to get out of it, as it did not and was not likely to pay the sufficient interest for the money involved.

He drew two lessons from this: first, outlets nearer home would be easier to manage and, secondly, it was the expanding working-class market that held out most prospects.

His resolve was strengthened by the realisation that his Lancaster trade was also suffering a period of stagnation in the early-1880s. Between 1881 and 1886 turnover at his Penny Street stores slumped, falling from approximately £8,605 to just £6,670. Some of this may have been due to the dislocation to trade caused by the fire of 1879–80 which destroyed nearly all his stock and forced him to trade temporarily from the nearby Exchange Hall in Penny Street. But it is significant that the Co-op, T. D.'s main rival, also experienced a period of stagnation at the same time, suggesting

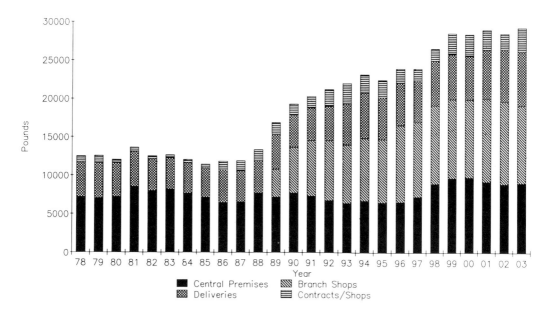

Figure 3: *The growth of trade, 1878–1903, as reflected in surviving account books*

that it was not a problem confined to T. D. Smiths.[4] Since Lancaster's population was rising at this time and prices were not falling dramatically, a fundamental change in the city's trading practices was obviously occurring to account for the decline.

The commercial trade directories of the early-1880s show that Penny Street and Cheapside were the main food shopping streets in Lancaster and that groceries and general provisions were sold by independent grocers and small shopkeepers. Over the following years, however, patterns of trade altered dramatically.[5] On the one hand, heightened competition from emerging multiples, very different creatures from the traditional, independent family grocer, posed a signficant threat to these shopkeepers from the 1890s. None of the grocers or tea dealers in Penny Street in Wells's trade directory of 1889 was a branch of a multiple chain; by 1912 Liptons, Home and Colonial, Maypole, and Slaters were all present. On the other hand, the number of small food retailing outlets in the town centre declined dramatically. The reason for this was that

small shops were moving out into the new working-class residential suburbs on the outskirts of town: the maturing freehold estate which had been growing steadily since the late-1850s and the new Primrose and Moorlands developments of the 1880s and 1890s to the east, the Marsh to the west, and the expanding township of Skerton on the north bank of the Lune. Here they could set up cheaply, either in purpose-built corner shops or crudely adapted front rooms of houses, and take advantage of people's tendency to shop in the immediate vicinity of their homes. Recognising that people were unlikely to visit the town centre for regular daily purchases, both Smith and the Co-op decided to take their shops to the people. So, soon after the Southport business had been disposed of, T. D. took a 'new departure':

by buying houses in the suburbs, in central positions, the [bottleneck] where the people must pass to get into the centre of the town and with a view of opening them as branch shops, for the more convenient distribution of goods, believing it to be wise to lay goods near to the

17

purchaser, and at the same time list prices as in the central shop.

These shops offered convenience to customers since they were situated much nearer to their homes, lessening the time and energy spent on the purchase of provisions. Strategically located on street corners, T. D. could command the trade of a whole area.

Over the next decade and a half, therefore, T. D. opened six suburban branches. The first of these was on West Road on the new Marsh estate, an existing property which was modified and opened for business in August 1888. A similar rebuilding followed the purchase of the premises on Owen Road, Skerton which opened in February 1889. Despite the fact that T. D. had been advised against this site, since the Co-op operated a successful branch around the corner 'share owned by many of the better artisans there', trade here expanded steadily over the next few years. A house was also bought and converted on the expanding Primrose estate at the corner of Dale Street and Bowerham Terrace and also one at the other end of the terrace 'to secure this against others who might buy it to oppose us'. This was opened in November 1888. After a short break, a further shop was opened on prominent site on the Freehold at the corner of Ullswater Road and Upper Moor Lane in 1895, Smith even buying the premises next door and converting them into another shop for let. This branch soon achieved the highest turnover of all the branches in the 1890s. The final documented expansion under T. D.'s control was into a small double-windowed shop on the corner of Dumbarton Road and Stirling Road in the new

Plate 4: *An advertisement emphasising value for money, c.1900*

Gregson or Moorlands estate in May 1898. The last branch in Bowerham village was opened sometime between 1903 and 1905.

The success of these branches must be seen as the major factor in explaining not only T. D.'s survival but his firm's reputation as Lancaster's largest and most prominent grocery business. Individually the branches enjoyed mixed fortunes; the Skerton shop, for example, suffered a downturn in trade by the early-1900s in the face of competition from the Co-op and the run-down of Lancaster waggon works, the chief employer in the area. Smith also complained of other shopkeepers who imitated him, often 'men who have previously been trained and in the employ of our own business', a threat he thought sufficiently serious to require employees 'to make it an agreement on entering our service, for them not to begin in opposition against us within a given time and within a certain radius'. But the huge increase in turnover after the expansion of the branch network is an indication of its general success. By 1900 income from the branches outstripped that from either his central premises or his deliveries, accounting for over £10,000 per annum, or between 30% to 40% of total turnover each year.

After this burst of activity the pace of expansion slowed considerably, partly because Lancaster itself ceased to develop at the same rate in the 20th century, partly as a result of E. G. Smith's conscious decision to consolidate. There was no further expansion until the inter-war years, and this was took the form of acquiring permanent rural branches to take over some of the responsibilities of the central store. In 1925 the firm took over the old-established business of W. & J. Mossop in Grange over Sands; in 1929 it acquired Crossfield's at Arnside, continuing to trade under that name in the area; in 1930 it opened a branch in Settle in modernised premises on the corner of Cheapside and Duke Street.[6] Although these shops then took over some of the deliveries previously organised from Lancaster, they only marginally extended the areas served by the firm.

Plate 5: *Owen Road, Skerton, prior to redevelopment of the area in the 1960s, showing T. D. Smith's branch shop (reproduced courtesy of Albert Gillham).*

Attitudes to business

Throughout the firm's history every generation of Smiths viewed the Co-operative movement as their main rival. Although T. D. resented the threat which smaller suburban shops and national multiples presented, he reserved his most forthright condemnation for the Co-op. Partly this was simply a case of straightforward competition since, like Smith, the Co-op responded to the changing retail conditions of the 1880s by opening branches throughout the district and offering extensive delivery services.[7] Like Smith the Co-op also emphasised the quality of its own brands and sought to cream off the reliable cash trade of the working class. But mingled with the potential threat was an intense dislike of, and contempt for,

everything which the Co-op stood for. This animosity carried itself over to infect the workforce and family members who were not directly involved in the business. Even today Ian Smith, great-grandson of T. D. Smith, confesses to feeling a 'slight sense of guilt' on going into a Co-op, or even 'one of those wicked multiples' since there was 'something nasty' about them all.[8] T. D. disagreed wholeheartedly with the Co-op's motto:

'Strive to increase the good of all;
Thus only can the share of each increase'.

Such a collective philosophy was anathema to the intense individualistic streak which ran through most private tradesmen like Smith. The Co-op, he argued, was an exploitative system, one which fooled customers into believing that they were buying quality goods at bargain prices

19

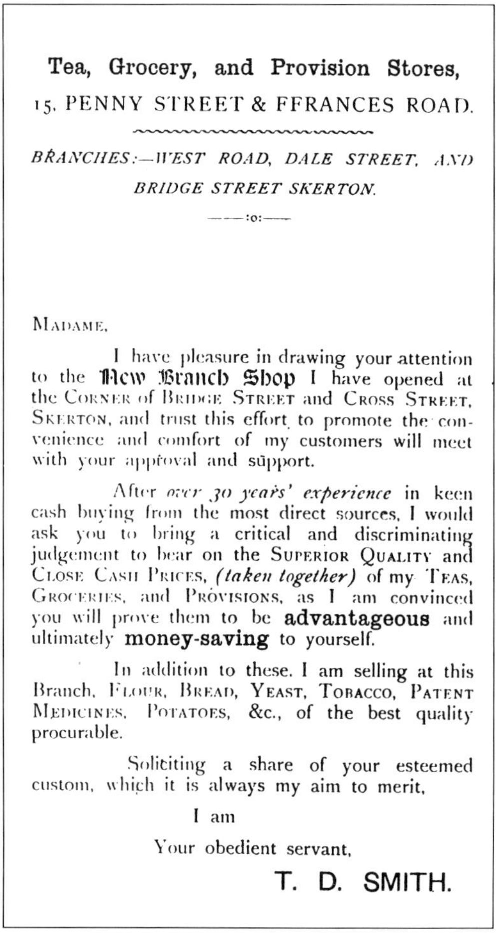
Tea, Grocery, and Provision Stores,

15, PENNY STREET & FFRANCES ROAD.

BRANCHES:—WEST ROAD, DALE STREET, AND BRIDGE STREET SKERTON.

—:o:—

MADAME,

I have pleasure in drawing your attention to the **New Branch Shop** I have opened at the CORNER of BRIDGE STREET and CROSS STREET, SKERTON, and trust this effort to promote the convenience and comfort of my customers will meet with your approval and support.

After *over 30 years' experience* in keen cash buying from the most direct sources, I would ask you to bring a critical and discriminating judgement to bear on the SUPERIOR QUALITY and CLOSE CASH PRICES, *(taken together)* of my TEAS, GROCERIES, and PROVISIONS, as I am convinced you will prove them to be **advantageous** and ultimately **money-saving** to yourself.

In addition to these, I am selling at this Branch, FLOUR, BREAD, YEAST, TOBACCO, PATENT MEDICINES, POTATOES, &c., of the best quality procurable.

Soliciting a share of your esteemed custom, which it is always my aim to merit,

I am

Your obedient servant,

T. D. SMITH.

Plate 6: *Circular announcing the opening of T. D. Smith's first branch shop at Skerton in 1889. Note the emphasis here on competitive cash prices for the working class.*

when in fact they were not. The quarterly 'divi' was nothing but a fraud since 'it has never recouped to the working man what has been taken out of him in the articles bought by their system in quality and price'. The Co-op was 'a selfish mode of trading', denying upright private shopkeepers business that was due to them, by playing on the greedy instincts of the customer.

Not surprisingly T. D. was a believer in the virtues of the private trader who

> with only his capital to depend on, cultivated himself and watched the markets most closely, and thus bought better all round than did co-operative buyers who were dealing in other people's money.

The successful private trader, he argued, not only provided a better service but represented all the business virtues: independence, probity, concern for the customer, knowledge of the trade. In common with many other men in his position at this time Smith felt that such skill and service deserved rather more public recognition than they received:

> Many an honest, honourable, hard working tradesman has been . . . named as extortionate middlemen and as a lower order of being. They have been much in evidence and looked up at election times, to do public work, church work and give money to all objects and to pay Social Taxes, Income and Imperial Taxes, without being regarded with deference and respect due to them . . .

He did not see why

> such men of education, character and ability should in any way rank in public estimate and society, as second to military, clergy or other professions, just because they are traders.

The private trader owed his success to his qualities, rather than any gimmicks. These certainly were the factors to which T. D., in common with many other businessmen, attributed his own prosperity. It was important 'in all business matters . . . to be the soul of honour, probity, honest and faithful'. 'Our rigid practice has been, all through our business career, to sell all goods for what they are . . . to give weight and measure in all transactions, but nothing more'. Even making allowance for an element of self-congratulation which runs through such autobiographies, it is clear that T. D. was a shrewd businessman who was able to spot openings in the market and capitalise on them. He knew his limits, however, and was careful never to overstretch himself. Being well aware of the dangers of trying to do too much on borrowed capital, he took

> great care not to rush after more business and lay out more money than I could manage and control, and commensurate with my capital.

The sight of contemporaries falling into debt and losing their businesses strengthened his determination to avoid heavy borrowing except for improvements to property. Rather than rely on the extended credit which was the backbone of much trade at the time, T. D. made a point of paying all his accounts on time. Prompt payment, he believed, increased creditors' confidence and secured him valuable discounts on purchases. He was equally concerned to be selective in the extended credit he offered to customers. This he offered only to those families in 'good medium positions', preferring in the main to trade on the quality of product, value for money and personal service. T. D.'s rule of thumb was simple: 'Stick to giving credit in business, to the extent of the capital in your business'.

T. D. also stressed the importance of knowing everything about his stock in trade. He believed it was essential to know exactly what stock he had at any one time so that he could gauge his orders accordingly. He also prided himself on knowing what, when and where to buy: 'to succeed in business, the buying part is a great part of the battle'. His strategy was to provide a wide range of goods at different prices and not to become too dependent on one sector of the market. There would always be, he observed, those who wanted high-class goods and those who wanted lower priced goods, although all would want 'an article that will give satisfaction . . . hence the importance of not descending too low in quality for the sake of price'. 'Shop at the stores that give you satisfaction and quality at prices you can afford' remained the firm's slogan throughout its history. Rather than price cutting, the business appealed primarily on the quality of its goods, and the service and expertise of its trained staff. These were the foundations of its success and it is to them that we now turn in greater detail.

Notes

1. P. Gooderson, 'The social and economic history of Lancaster, 1780–1914', Unpublished Ph.D. Thesis, University of Lancaster (1975), pp. 372–94.
2. Lancaster City Reference Library; Account Books 1877–1903, MS 8065. All subsequent details on turnover are from this source.
3. T. D. himself is unsure in his autobiography of the precise date of the fire.
4. Turnover in 1878 was £56,826; in 1885 it had dropped to £48,254. For full details see *Lancaster: A Souvenir of the 48th Co-operative Congress, 1916,* (CWS, Manchester, 1916), p. 140.
5. Trade directories consulted were P. Mannex and Co., *Topography and Directory of Lancaster and Seven Miles Around,* (Preston, 1881); Wells, *Lancaster District Directory,* (Shrewsbury, 1889); W. J. Cook and Co., *Lancaster, Morecambe and District Directory* (Lancaster, 1899); T. Bulmer and Co., *History, Topography and Directory of Lancaster and District* (Preston, 1912).
6. Press cutting in the family's scrapbook, 1933, possibly *The Grocer;* these details differ slightly from those in the programme printed for the centenary celebrations in 1958.
7. W. A. Smith, *A History of the Origin and Progress of Lancaster and Skerton Equitable Industrial Co-operative Society Limited* (1891), p. 52.
8. Interview with Ian Smith, 8 May 1990.

For Our Fighting Heroes

Only the Best is good enough.
You always get it at

T. D. Smith's Stores.

WE are constantly receiving letters acknowledging the safe arrival of parcels sent by us for customers to friends at the front, in the Navy, and to interned Prisoners. In many are valued suggestions as to what is really most appreciated; every week sees some new and useful articles added to our stock, and we shall welcome any further suggestions.

The Mono Service Vessel—lined with impervious sterile glaze—strong and light, for filling with Butter, Cheese, Jam, etc., ½lb. & 1lb. size, **1d.**, 2lb. size, **1½d.**

Sardines in oil or tomatoes, patent opener tins, **2½d.**, **4½d.**, **6d.**, **7½d.**, **9d.** (boneless) **1/- and 1/4½.**

Wensleydale Cheese.—Rich and ripe, 8—10lbs. weight. **1/-** per lb., Wensley Midgets, **1/6** each. Lactic Cheese in **3½d.** and **6½d.** drums.

Harris' Noted Wilts.—Sliced Ham, **2/-**; Pork Sausages, **1/4**; Camp Pies, **1/4** per tin, etc., all ready cooked.

Radium Pocket Stoves—much appreciated. 12 hot drinks for **4d.**

Beaches' Dessert Fruits in tins. Strawberries, **1/3**; Raspberries. **1/3**; Greengages, **1/3**; Victoria Plums, **1/-**; Fruit Salad, **1/-** and **1/6.**

Oxford Coated Parchment Puddings.—Just the Xmas Pudding to send to the boy—each **10½d.**

Tongues in patent opening tins, **10½d.**, **1/5**, **2/8**, **3/-**, and **3/6.**

Horlick's Malted Milk Tablets—plain or chocolate flavoured—per flask **5½d.** and **10½d.**

Tea Tablets.—Sufficient for 50 good cups of Tea, per tin, **7d.** Cocoa and Milk Tablets, **1d.** each.

Biscuits in Special Tins.—Royal Assorted, **1/3**; Thin Arrowroot. **2/-**; Ginger Nuts, **2/2**; Wheatmeal, **1/10**; Rich Mixed. **2/8**; Special Heroes' Box, **1/7½**; Empire Box, **2/-**, etc., etc.

Plum Puddings, ready cooked in basins — our special recipe—**1/-**, **1/4½**, **1/10½**, and **2/4½.**

Dessert Fruits in special wood drums, several varieties, **7d.** and **1/-**.

Cafe au Lait	per tin	**6d.**
Cocoa and Milk	„	**4½d.**
Richest Cream	„	**4½d. & 6½d.**
Oxo Cubes, 6 large cups	„	**6d.**
C. & B. Pressed Beef	„	**2/3**
Diploma Milk (lever tops)	„	**7d.**
Tuna Fish, very delicious	„	**6½d. & 9½d.**
Plasmon Biscuits	„	**1/- & 2/3**
Scotch Oatcakes	„	**8½d.**
Finest Crab	„	**11d.**
Herrings in Tomato Sauce	„	**5d.**
Asparagus	„	**1/2**
Green Peas, large size	„	**10½d.**
Curried Fowl		**1/-**
Steak and Kidney Puddings	„	**1/5**
Baked Beans in Tomato Sauce	„	**7d. & 10½d.**
Finest Salmon, large tins		**7d., 8d. & 9d.**
Marmalade, in tins	1lb.	**6d.**
Lobster, in tins		**8d. & 1/-**
Slade's Toffee, all kinds, ...	per tin	**6½d.**
Butter Scotch, per lb., **6d.**; 7lb. tins,		**3/3**
Finest Boiled Sweets, ...	per lb.	**8d.**
Old Fashioned Peppermints,	per lb.	**1/-**
Plain Chocolate in large variety.		
Cakes in large variety, from **6d per lb.**		
Lemon Cheese, ...	per jar,	**4d. & 7d.**
Beef and Tongue, ...	per mould,	**1/6**
Noel's Potted Meats, ...	per jar,	**6½d.**
Condensed Milk, full cream, 1lb.		**6d.**
Luscious Dessert Raisins, ...	per lb.	**10d.**
Scotch Oatmeal, all cuts, ...	per lb.	**2½d.**
Concentrated Soups, all kinds,	per packet,	**1½d. & 2d.**
Spices (pepper, salt, etc.), recommended for interned prisoners		
Finest Carbolic Soap, ...	per lb.	**4d.**

If desired we shall be glad to pack in free boxes and send according to Official directions to any of our customers' friends at the Front.

T. D. SMITH'S Stores,

17 & 19, PENNY STREET AND SUBURBAN BRANCHES, LANCASTER.

BEELEY BROS., PRINTERS, PENNY STREET.

Plate 7: *Like most grocers T. D. Smiths offered to send provisions to troops at the front in the First World War. This price list presumably includes those items which were considered most appropriate or were most in demand. Note the 'tea tablets'.*

3

The nature of trade

WHEN you entered the doors of T. D. Smith's you stepped into another world.[1] A pungent blend of roasted coffee, tea, spices, and polished wood greeted the customer, along with a welcome from the assistants, each standing behind their own marble counters.

The central shop itself in the 20th century was divided into a provisions side and a grocery side, with each product having its place. At the main shop on Penny Street there was a bottling room for jams, vinegar and other preserves, a room for cases of fruit and dried goods and a paper room for bags, string and Smith's distinctive white wrapping paper with its blue teapot printed on it, the trade sign for which it was noted throughout the district. There were five floors to the premises including the cellar, and at the back of the shop was a hoist to all floors and a platform for the loading and unloading of goods. The manager's office was on the first floor. Before the alterations of the mid-1930s there was another office at the back of the shop for taking orders by telephone. The accounts and other business records were also kept in the office. The firm also took pride in their prominent window displays on Penny Street, the job of dressing the window being designated to the grocery or provisions manager or a top assistant. Each product on display had to be clearly ticketed and the price alternatives shown.

Although the general consensus amongst employees was that the adjoining Ffrances Passage shop was for the 'poorer customers', and that the main shop in Penny Street attracted the better class of shopper, this opinion was not held by either E. G. or F. B. Smith, who, in their writings, stressed that customers came from very varied backgrounds, purchasing goods from both shops. Many of these ex-customers still today fondly recall the friendly atmosphere and the wide variety of products sold, describing T. D. Smiths as a 'wonderful shop'. There were high-backed stools in the shop for customers to rest while their orders were being assembled and the customers' children were often given biscuits. Similar practices were maintained as late as the 1960s and 1970s. The assistants would pack customers' shopping bags and, if they were delivering to the house, they would carry the provisions right into the customers' homes rather than simply leaving them on the doorstep. Unlike some other shops, there was no charge for these deliveries; it was all part of the service. In addition, in later years, food which had already been bought would be kept in the refrigerator while the customers did the rest of their shopping elsewhere.

The grocery trade changed considerably over the lifespan of the shop, reflecting the opening up of new international sources of supply, developments in preservation and packaging, and the increasing ability of customers to afford more varied goods. An individual grocer's range of stock also reflected his size and the market in which he traded, some mid-19th-century shops like Woods and Bromley, which stood on Horseshoe Corner, even combining grocery with apparently incongruous trades like ironmongery. As befitted a high-class grocer, however, T. D. Smiths boasted that, through them, 'the world's produce is delivered to your door in perfect condition'. Tea, spices, nuts, dried fruits, flour, butter, cheese, provisions, soap and household goods were always staples of the trade but T. D.'s also sold unusual products. Although some of these were only available seasonally or at Christmas, the firm's catalogue for 1937, sent to all customers on request, posed the question, 'How can we get something different?' and provided the answer: 'Consult T. D. Smiths who are experts in providing exclusive goods for particular people'. A 'selection' of their specialities available all the year round followed and included such delicacies as glass bottled prawns, anchovy rings, caviare and olives; tinned Bombay Duck, mackerels in wine, whole chickens and oysters; fruit juices and exotic biscuits. Rationing during and after the war severely restricted the range available but as it came to an end in the early-1950s a full range of delicacies was reintroduced.

Many goods continued to be sold loose, or packed on the premises under T. D. Smith's own brand right until the firm's closure. Increasingly, however, pre-packaged goods appeared on the shelves, including biscuits, cakes, breakfast cereals, chocolates, cocoa, speciality sweets, pickles, sauces, soups, tinned fruit, vegetables, milk. processed meats, jams, patent medicines, soaps and soap powders, and were sold under nationally advertised brand names which emerged from the late-19th century. If a customer desired something which the shop did not stock, the management would do its utmost to get it for the following week. Variety was complemented in the provisions department with freshness. 'Our immense turnover', boasted one advertise-ment, 'enables us to offer every variety of

Plate 8: *The shop's display of Christmas crackers and specialities, probably in the 1930s, but which was a regular feature until closure in 1961*

provision day-by-day in the freshest condition and of the choicest quality'.[2]

When it came to buying supplies for his shops, T. D.'s philosophy was 'a thing well bought is half sold' and, as we have seen, he made great efforts to obtain access to national suppliers at the outset. The shop drew its supplies from a wide range of sources and was visited by travellers who came armed with sample products to obtain orders. Manchester and Liverpool were always important centres for many provisions: lard, coffee, dried and tinned fruit and biscuits. London was always the hub of the tea market. The railway was vital in the transportation of these supplies. Produce like salt was delivered to Lancaster station and then transported by Smiths' own waggons to the central Penny Street depot for breaking into saleable lumps. Sometimes the rail company used their own road vehicles to deliver right up to the yard at the back of the shop, this service being included in the price of the goods.

Although meat provisions like bacon were increasingly bought from recognised suppliers like Harris because they had to be thoroughly examined and cured before sale, some produce was bought locally. Where dairy products were concerned, a neat and amicable agreement existed between farming customers and the grocer with cheeses and butter sometimes being bought at the farmhouses from the firm's customers or at market. In the 1930s some sixty dozen eggs each week were purchased this way.

Many products were partially processed or packed on the premises and sold as T. D. Smiths' own brand. Vinegar, jam and treacle, for example, were bottled in the shop, and Herbert Pyke, who spent all his working life with the firm from 1930, recalls that during his apprenticeship customers received a penny for large jars and a halfpenny for small ones which they returned. Currants and other dried fruits were bought loose and had to be weighed out by hand. Butter was another product which was weighed and wrapped on the premises. Tea was blended in a room above the shop;

bacon boned and sliced in the white-tiled cellars below. At the shop at Grange, a bakehouse was attached which used to produce the finest shortbread made with butter and eggs bought from the farming customers which were not quite of saleable quality. Cheeses were stored in racks at the central shop and turned frequently while they matured, the job of tasting them usually being reserved for the proprietor himself. Smith's own branded products, however, were not restricted to staple items or local produce. One unusual offering which was advertised around the turn of the century, was his 'Lactaline', 'a harmless and effectual preservative for milk, cream, butter and meat.' It was sold in ¼ lb, ½ lb and 1lb packets at a price of 1s. 4d a pound. 'One pennyworth', it was claimed, could keep 'eight gallons of milk sweet for three days in the hottest weather'. As pre-packed branded goods from national suppliers gradually crept into the markets, fewer and fewer products were packed and processed on the premises, but Smiths continued to emphasise their own brands, which were often rather cheaper but always of good quality, right up to the end.

T. D. Smiths were most renowned for, and prided themselves on, their distinctive blending of tea. This dated back to the expertise which T. D. acquired during his apprenticeship when he 'was bent on forming a knowledge of the quality of the goods handled, the origin, growth, manipulation, value, blending and distribution' of tea. His training gave him

the opportunity of tasting teas, forming a practical knowledge of the various characteristics of the various China teas, their effect and proportion upon blends, and forming an acquaintance of the public tastes and popular wants.

In common with other grocers, he embraced the opportunities offered by the appearance of Indian and Ceylon teas in the late-19th century to cash in on an expanding market. T. D. soon prided himself on producing a range of blends of Indian, Ceylon and China tea by personally selecting 'those teas which excel in purity, fine flavour and great strength, and which especially suit this water'. At one time Smiths sold 32 different types of tea to suit all tastes and pockets. Training in this formed an important part of the workers' apprenticeship, but the initial blending and tasting itself was usually carried out by the proprietor himself. The room where this was done in later years was positioned above the front shop in Penny Street and Ian Smith, son of the last proprietor, Francis Brian Smith, remembers being met from school by his father and taken back to this office where there would be a line of some forty teacups and small teapots for brewing the blend, and a receptacle at the end of the table for collecting the samples, for such tea was never swallowed but merely savoured on the palate. Here, he would watch his father meticulously sampling each tea individually. The firm produced a special price list with a detailed description of all the types of teas sold and a leaflet entitled *Hints on Tea Making* was sent to customers, courtesy of the firm. The shop also housed an extensive collection of decorated tea tins and boxes for sale. Around the turn of the century a Japanese decorated tin for holding 3lbs of tea, for example, could be bought for 9d. Other items included Japanese teapots, Tete-à-Tete teasets, and coffee and cocoa jugs. Free gifts were occasionally given with tea: a special engraved coronation tea tray was presented to every customer who bought a pound of either Coronation or Jubilee tea in 1937.

An extensive mail order business for Smiths' teas also seems to have existed if his advertisements are anything to go by. One such advertisement contained a section from a customer's letter which read, 'Will Messrs. Smith please send 3lb of their 1/10d tea to the address [Switzerland] enclosed? My daughters say they do so enjoy it as they can get no tea like it on the Continent'. Another similar request came from Bavaria. How this was squared with claims that the teas were specially blended for local water is not mentioned.

Coffee was another speciality of the firm.

Back in the 1850s and 1860s T. D. recalls that 'the coffees of that day were mostly Plantation Ceylon, with a small import of Jamaica'. As prices rose in the later decades of the century coffee was planted 'in many parts of the world, Central and South America, Rio, Santas, Uganda'. Unlike tea, however, demand did not rise as quickly and there was, T. D. observed, 'a decided plethora and over production of coffee' that 'brought down prices to such a low level as to be ruinous to the companies involved in the culture of it'. Despite this price fall, demand for coffee never paralleled that of tea, but it comprised an important part of T. D.'s quality trade. Coffee was freshly roasted and ground daily on the premises in the Ffrances Passage shop. People always knew when coffee was being roasted as the smell used to drift into the street. Herbert Pyke recalls how sometimes the belt which drove the coffee roasting machine would stick, causing the coffee to burn. The first he would know of this would be when customers rushed into the shop crying 'the coffee is on fire!' The coffee department also provided instructions as to how to make good coffee. Unlike tea, the firm did not recommend buying it in large quantities or storing it for any length of time: 'They ask the co-operation of their customers in their endeavours to secure the greater popularity of this beneficial beverage by procuring their coffee as often as possible in small quantities, grinding it when possible in their own mills'.

T. D. Smiths employed a variety of techniques to promote their products. Writing in 1937 F. B. Smith explained that there were

two distinct types of appeal, one addressed to the customer for whom the highest quality is more important than the price, and the other addressed to the customer to whom price is of first importance.[3]

This meant that blanket advertising in the local press was rarely appropriate except for special lines or seasonal produce. Instead the firm devised specific material and approaches for different classes of customers. Flysheets and posters circulated for the branches emphasised value for money: 'Make your money go twice as far', or 'Shillings saved means pounds in the bank'. Another method whereby Smiths promoted their own products was by free samples and special offers, sending small samples of tea to customers, for example, or, as rationing ended in the 1950s, promoting cheeses during special sampling weeks when customers were invited to taste the sixty varieties sold in the shop.[4] At Christmas special promotional leaflets were issued listing seasonal stock, boasting by the 1930s, for example, to have 'the largest selection of crackers in the North'. A separate alcove on the premises was always decked out with a tempting array of seasonal products. The shop also had a Christmas club. Details of how this worked around the turn of the century which have survived show that each member paid in regularly between 1st September and 1st December and could then draw on it during the first two weeks of December, after which time the club was closed, a clear attempt to encourage people to shop early and spread the Christmas rush over a longer period. 'To prove that the promoter reaps no advantage from the members, beyond the ordinary profit on goods sold' 5% *per annum* interest was added to the sum paid in by the members. Up until 1889 T. D. had also adopted the common practice of giving away a free gift to his customers at Christmas time. In that year, however, he resolved to:

> discontinue the custom of giving Almanacks as Christmas gifts this year . . . they have not been esteemed by the receiver, and but little value place on them, indeed, though in the aggregate of great cost to the giver, I am afraid they have more frequently been the cause of offence than otherwise.

Instead he donated the money saved to the Royal Albert Asylum and new Lancaster Infirmary, a praiseworthy public gesture but one which was possibly also intended to increase his chances of obtaining some of their lucrative contract business.

Plate 9: *A rare offer of a free gift, to celebrate George VI's coronation. Special tea blends were also produced for this and for George V's jubilee.*

By far the most effective form of advertising was direct mailing. In addition to supplying regular customers with a full price catalogue of the shop's entire stock and annual Christmas lists, in the 1930s the firm also sent out *The Housewives' Guide*, a monthly booklet announcing new products, drawing attention to special offers, reminding customers of seasonal lines, providing household tips and cooking recipes. It even included a children's page and gardening notes. F. B. Smith considered this 'the most remunerative form of advertising we have ever attempted . . . and we would strongly recommend those of our fellow grocers who feel that there is no future for the private trader to adopt similar methods'.[5]

As we have seen, however, T. D. Smiths did not just seek to attract people into its shops. For many customers, much of the shop's appeal lay in the extensive delivery network which enabled them to shop from the comfort of their homes. This network consisted of a regular pattern of timetabled deliveries to local suburbs and outlying rural areas. In 1910, for example, the firm's printed catalogue shows that there were three despatches to all areas of Lancaster at 10.30am, 2.30pm and 6.30pm every day except Wednesday. In addition, Lancaster's residents were advised that 'where desired, our town representative would wait upon customers at a regular hour to suit their convenience'. In the country areas the firm's travellers would call regularly on specified days to take orders and payment for the previous purchases, and the goods would be delivered later the same week. Customers in Bolton-le-Sands, Hest Bank and Slyne, for example, were visited on Tuesdays, their orders delivered on Thursday. Those further up the Lune Valley, at Tunstall and Leck, were visited on Wednesday and their goods were delivered on Saturday. The frequency of this service depended on the area but everywhere it improved by the 1930s. Around the turn of the century, areas close to Lancaster were visited fortnightly, those more distant, monthly, or in the case of Hellifield, Long Preston and Chapel le Dale, bi-monthly. By the 1930s, with the increasing use of motor transport and the opening of shops at Grange and Settle, which took responsibility for deliveries in their own areas, everywhere was visited more frequently.

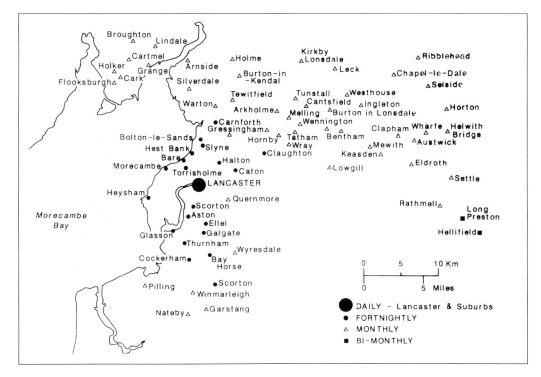

Figure 4: *T. D. Smith's delivery network around 1910 as operated from the central Lancaster stores. From the 1930s the shops at Grange and Settle took over deliveries to some of the outlying districts.*

28

Areas close to Grange enjoyed twice-weekly deliveries, and the area around Settle fortnightly calls. Only the more distant or inaccessible places in the Pennine fells were left with monthly visits (see figure 4). When James Redmayne, who began work with the firm on leaving school in 1932, took to travelling in 1948 there were three travellers operating from the main Lancaster shop, covering an area stretching from Silverdale, Carnforth and Bolton-le-Sands to the north, Ingleton and Bentham to the east and Garstang and Wyresdale to the south.

Such a complex delivery service required effective organisation if it was to run successfully. In 1937, in an article in *Grocery*, F. B. Smith explained in detail how this was achieved. Each traveller reported to his branch or head office every morning and evening to place his orders and to collect any special instructions or messages which may have come through while he was out on his circuit. A chart in the head office depicted the traveller's calls showing 'at a glance the exact position of any man at any time, thereby enabling us to get in touch with him if he is wanted urgently'. Orders were taken on specially printed itemised forms, bound in books in duplicate so that a copy of the order could be left with the customer as a reminder. Even the colour of these was distinctive to ensure easy recognition and identification.

Smiths offered the delivery service by their own vans free of charge, 'carriage paid to our customer's door'. Additional orders at other times were also sent carriage paid if they were above a certain value. The catalogue for 1910 advertised:

> Country orders of 15/- value are sent carriage paid either by rail or carrier within 25 miles radius. Carriage paid on general orders of £1. 10s and upwards within fifty miles per luggage train; for £5 and upwards to any Railway Station in England, Scotland or Wales.

In the 1950s, however, as the cost of deliveries became more difficult to justify as prices of goods became more competitive and large profit margins out of which the delivery service was financed, were eroded, Francis Brian Smith considered charging for regular deliveries. Even this was shortlived since custom declined still further as a result, so he resorted once again to free delivery. Nevertheless, the area covered continued to dwindle until James Redmayne recalls that he was delivering only to Quernmore, Halton, Cocker-

Plate 10: *'Deliveries in the winter'. Jim Redmayne's photograph shows his van on the moors above Roeburndale in the 1960s. A shovel was always carried in the van.*

29

ham and Glasson. In 1966 all travelling out of town ceased, the volume of business no longer justifying the expenses involved.

In the firm's early years deliveries had been made by horse and cart, a centenary article of 1958 recalling that 'a fleet of smart ponies and their vehicles known as Smith's Pony Expresses are still remembered by many Lancastrians'.[6] Errand boys on foot or bicycles were used for short distance deliveries in town, as even the branch shops delivered. In the countryside, representatives initially travelled by rail and then walked or later cycled between farmhouses, but by the 1920s motorcycles were regularly used, sometimes doubling as delivery vehicles. Many goods, however, continued to be sent by rail. Thirty or forty boxes at a time might be sent from Green Ayre station to Hornby or Bentham where they would be met by a local farmer with a horse and cart who would then deliver the goods. By the 1930s, the firm had a fleet of 30-cwt. vans which covered some 50,000 miles a year delivering to customers.[7] After this time motor vans were increasingly used by travellers as well who also took on the responsibility for deliveries. James Redmayne recalls of his experiences in the 1950s, 'the little van used to be absolutely packed to the ceiling when I set off; it's a wonder I didn't get pulled up for being overweight'. Orders had to be delivered whatever the weather. In winter skid-chains and snow tyres were used to get across the higher ground: 'you just had to go and hope for the best'. There was a lot of co-operation between farmers and travellers. During bad weather when travellers could not get through, farmers would distribute the goods themselves. Relations between customers and travellers, therefore, were informal and friendly.

Just as the central shop in Lancaster attracted customers from a variety of back-grounds, so too did the delivery service. James Redmayne remembers delivering to the Earl of Sefton when he lived at Abbeystead, and it is highly likely that royalty was entertained here with T. D. Smith's goods. Norman Bradley recalls

'really massive orders' being packed in the warehouse at the back of the shop when shooting parties were in residence. At the opposite end of the scale deliveries were also made to the poorer classes, even to the home for unmarried mothers, but nevertheless, 'you just had to treat them the same . . . their money was as good as the others'!' Some customers placed very small orders but for the traveller everyone had to be treated respectfully and equally, no matter how much or how little they spent.

The traveller was more than a simple taker of orders. He was responsible for drumming up trade. 'If you got the farmer and you were well in there you were nearly certain to have the staff as well', recalls Mr Redmayne. Whenever there was a special offer on, the traveller would collect the usual order first and then attempt to promote the additional sample product. In this way, the original order would not be lost. As it was felt that the traveller knew the needs of the customers better than the head office, F. B. Smith felt that 'we find it best to leave the choice, or at any rate recommendation, of the special line to the individual customer'.[8]

Only the two world wars disrupted this pattern of trade. As well as depriving the firm of most of its experienced male staff, turnover was also considerably reduced by shortages and rationing, and deliveries restricted to large orders due to the ration-ing of petrol during the Second World War. Almost every basic item in the shop was rationed during the 1940s, one exception being coffee, as so few people in Britain drank it at the time. Customers had to register with a particular shop and buy all products from that retailer. It was not possible to buy butter at the Co-op for example, and tea at T. D. Smiths. A certain number of ration tickets were guaranteed by the government for products such as butter, tea and sugar and, in addition, a points system existed for the purchase of tinned foods whereby the customer could choose whether to buy, for example, corned beef or stewed figs. This points system also applied to fruit and vegetables when they were available.

Ensuring the smooth running of all this during a time when staff numbers were depleted was often difficult. The firm found that it was unable to meet all the demand for registrations, a letter sent to all customers explaining that:

> Owing to our desire to serve to the best of our ability . . . we regret we are unable to accept new registrations except in very special circumstances, nor are we able to accept registrations for a single commodity.

The sorting of the ration coupons was a lengthy and labour-intensive process. Although the firm had a large office staff Ian Smith remembers how his father used to bring home boxes of coupons for the children to count. As many as five or six thousand had to be cut out and counted in the evening.

According to Ian Smith his mother stuck rigidly to her rations on principle; 'never having an egg or ounce of butter more than [the family] were entitled to', but they eked out their supplies by keeping hens in their garden on Haverbreaks. After the war, however, Mrs Brian Smith found that she was given little credit for her honesty by her friends, and Ian recalls his father returning home with an extra pound of butter or sugar on a number of occasions which were then often used to bake cakes for friends of the family. E. G. Smith was also not averse to supplementing his stock on the side. Herbert Pyke recalls that after the war, while jam was still scarce, Edward, who had effectively retired from business then, used to come into the shop and be seen 'sidling up to the fixtures, trying to get hold of a jar and putting it into his pocket'!

Only after 1952 when rationing was gradually eliminated were T. D. Smiths able to resume their traditional patterns of trading. For those like Norman Bradley who trained with the firm during rationing but then had a break in National Service, the world of the 1950s was a very different place. Based upon the principles of 'Quality and Reliability', the firm embraced the removal of such restrictions on trade and resumed its extensive service, the nature of which had remained largely unaltered over the decades. By the mid-1950s, however, declining profit margins and changing patterns of trade were beginning to threaten its viability by undermining the emphasis on personal service which had sustained it for so long.

Notes

1. Much of the unattributed information for this chapter comes from miscellaneous 19th- and early 20th-century ephemera connected with the business stored in Lancaster City Library, MS 8066 & 8067 and from interviews with ex-employees: Herbert and Annie Pyke, 14 February 1990; James Redmayne, 15 March 1990; Thomas Seddon and Lesley Jones, 7 March 1990; Norman Bradley, 7 March 1991; and with the grandson of the original proprietor, Ian Smith, 8 May 1990.
2. Catalogues for c.1899 and 1910, MS 8066. A catalogue for 1937 in the possession of Mr. James Redmayne has also been consulted.
3. F. B. Smith, 'How We Operate On a Thirty Mile Radius', *Grocery*, June 1937.
4. Unopened sample packets have survived in the collection in Lancaster City Library, MS 8066.
5. F. B. Smith, *op. cit.*.
6. *Lancaster Guardian*, 27 June 1958.
7. Article in family scrapbook, possibly *The Grocer*, 1933.
8. F. B. Smith, *op. cit.*.

4

Working for T. D. Smiths

TO WORK for T. D. Smiths was to work for one of the most 'prestigious firms' in Lancaster according to past employee, James Redmayne.[1] The grocery trade offered regular employment, and jobs in it were eagerly sought after. For some employees, the trade was a natural choice as men simply followed their fathers' footsteps, but for others its appeal lay in the skilled nature of the business, preserved through an apprenticeship system that seemed to offer the prospects of secure, well paid employment.

Although T. D. Smiths were to become major employers, numbers at first were small. Initially T. D. ran the business with just the help of his sister, an errand boy and, before their children were born and the family ceased to live above the shop, his wife. As he expanded T. D. adopted the system, common in retailing at the time, of boarding assistants with the family. By 1871, the cramped living accommodation in Penny Street housed T. D., his wife and four young children, a domestic servant, nursemaid, traveller/grocer's assistant and two teenage apprentices. All except the domestic servant originated from Smith's home area. One of them, William Oldfield from Wray, is later known to have established his own business in the town with shops in St. Nicholas Street and on the Primrose estate.[2] Living-in ended soon after this when T. D.'s family moved into their own house in the suburbs and the numbers employed grew. By the early 1880s the business employed ten men and three boys [3] and, with the expansion of the branch network in the 1890s, the number

had risen to over thirty by the beginning of the century. As business became more complex, so did the variety of jobs. There were travellers to take orders; delivery men; stable hands to care for the horses and carts; warehousemen; specialist counter hands; office staff; errand boys, and apprentices. The continuing emphasis on service maintained this core number until the late-1950s, by which time there were also part-timers, usually women, on the payroll. Combined with the employees at Grange, Settle and Arnside, the firm had upwards of eighty staff by the time of its centenary celebrations in 1958.[4]

Grocery remained a predominantly male occupation for most of this time. Proprietors were invariably men in the 19th century, women being confined to small-scale general shopkeeping.[5] Their role as assistants was equally limited. In the years before the First World War, Smiths did not employ any women except T. D.'s eldest daughter, Eva, whose job consisted of

> the keeping of the cash book and posting of the same, the advising and keeping of the branch shop accounts, the invoicing and checking of the travellers' country books, the payment and keeping of petty cash, the writing up of the family retail book, the receipt of and the checking of cash takings . . .

Eva, T. D. observed, deserved 'great credit' for her 'correctness, if not for speed' in this tedious work.

With the outbreak of war in 1914 many men left their jobs and went away to fight for their country. Empty spaces desperately needed to be filled and the growth of female employment was the result. All of Smiths' fully fit, adult male workforce, including family members, signed up, and women were taken on for the first time, often being given the management of branch shops with little or no training. After the war, however, as men returned, few of these new female employees remained in the trade and between the wars their role continued to be confined to the office. Mrs Annie Pyke, for example, who began working for Smiths in 1934, worked from 8.00am until 6.00pm and 'mainly operated the order and credit system and stocktaking' in the office.[6] Only after the Second World War did women increasingly appear behind the counter and, even then, often only as part-time workers. By 1960 the majority of staff was female, although, with the exception of two experienced ladies who ran the Moorlands branch and tended to treat it as their own business, permanent and better paid positions continued to be held by men.

The firm took considerable care in the appointment and training of its staff. F. B. Smith explained the policy in 1937:

> . . . all our staff receive a thorough training at Head Office before their appointment to positions in the shops or on the road. Most of them grow up in the business and as soon as they have completed their apprenticeship training we send them away for a year or more to a leading grocery house in another town, to allow them to learn other methods, broaden their outlook generally and gain valuable experience of trade. Then, if they wished to return to their own town after a year or two's absence – and they usually do – we take them on as asssistants, promoting them according to their character and ability.

Choosing the right man as a traveller was particularly important: 'since customers often only see him, he represents the firm'. Such a man had to be

> absolutely reliable in every way . . . of strong character, high principle and pleasing personality. He must be adaptable . . . Even when we have selected our

man we do not appoint him to the position until he has had time to make sure that he really likes the job and we have had an opportunity to satisfy ourselves that he is fitted for it.[7]

A major feature of the firm's policy was its four-year apprenticeship system. During this period the trainee learned all about the grocer's stock in trade, the art of selling and how to treat customers politely. Through it the business retained its reputation for quality and service and embedded employee loyalty in the firm's culture.

To appreciate what this involved, it is best to draw on the experiences of former employees. For those like James Redmayne, who began working there soon after leaving school in 1932, the first tasks involved running errands and doing odd jobs such as cleaning windows and helping staff. Herbert Pyke, who started two years earlier, has vivid memories of what this could involve. His first job was to make his working apron out of an old sack, then:

> On a Monday morning I had to wash the windows and do all sorts of odd jobs. After this I had to go into the warehouse and help to assemble orders. I was really at everyone's beck and call. After six months I was moved to one of the branch shops, Ullswater Road; here I would collect and deliver orders. On a Thursday morning I would work at the main shop in the flour room, weighing flour and putting it into bags. In the afternoon I had to fill bottles with vinegar and cork and seal them . . . [other jobs included] mixing flour . . . cleaning fruit . . . Also I had to fill bottles with syrup. In winter the syrup was solid so one would have to leave a bottle under the barrel, turn on the tap and leave it whilst doing something else . . . of course one would forget about it and the syrup would go everywhere.

All apprentices were moved around the branches to give them a broad and varied experience under different managers. James Redmayne remembers working in West Road and Ullswater Road before spending more time at Bowerham, by then the busiest of the branches. Members of the

Plate 11: *The frontage of T. D. Smith's shop in Penny Street after modernisation, c.1937.*

family were not excluded from this and had to go through the same stages of training and were sent to different firms to gain experience.[8]

In 1909 the Institute of Certified Grocers had laid down a standard form of apprenticeship, validated by a system of examinations, to ensure that quality was maintained. Although it was not compulsory, employees were encouraged to follow its training and take the exams and the firm was prepared to pay the fees. Another long-term employee, Tommy Seddon, remembers that the night classes were taught at the Storey Institute before the final exam was taken in London. Herbert Pyke recalls his experience:

> a preliminary year, then three years studying the grocers' syllabus. Three stages were essential, intermediate first then associate of the Grocers Institute and finally member of the Grocers Institute. Oral and practical exams were necessary which involved the recognition of produce etc.

After completing their apprenticeship, assistants could often find their jobs becoming more specialist. Sidney Daley, for example, spent most of his working life on the cheese counter; Mr. Heywood,

recalls Ian Smith, was strictly 'the Bacon'.

Incentives and rewards for employees were offered from the early days of the firm. Prizes for good behaviour and long years of service are the most prominent examples. At the annual dinner in March 1907, for example, nine 'Cookson Prizes' of ten shillings and upwards were awarded to juniors for 'punctuality, good conduct and increased ability over the year'.[9] Norman Bradley recalls that he and other young trainees were rewarded with a day's outing to Cadbury's factory at Bournville, transported there with assistants from all over the north of England on Cadbury's specially chartered train. At the firm's centenary dinner in 1958, Mrs. Brian Smith presented clocks to eight employees who had given over twenty-five years' service to the firm.[10]

The emphasis on the quality of staff training, service and presentation reinforced Smiths' reputation as a high-class grocery store. The printed instructions to employees entering the firm's service also stressed the importance of selling quality produce and giving full measure. Politeness and respect towards customers was always stressed. Staff would never greet customers by their christian names. All

34

staff were to be smart and to wear an apron which they provided themselves. Different coloured aprons were appropriate to different counters. In summer top buttons were to remain fastened and ties straight. Ian Smith recalls Mr. Heywood always wearing a stiff, white, winged collar shirt. F. B. Smith always wore a suit, but when behind the counter put on an apron with a bib. Mr. Seddon recalls how one employee had his hair cut but because it was so short F. B. would not allow him to serve in the shop and so he was sent to the warehouse. Presentation and the image of the shop were of crucial importance.

For most of the firm's existence long opening hours were also part of the service. Before the First World War the shops opened at 8.00am every morning and remained open until 7.30pm on Monday, Tuesday and Thursday, 9.00pm on Friday and 10.00pm on Saturday. Only on Wednesdays did they close early, at 1.00pm. At Christmas the shops' closing hour was regularly 10.00pm or 11.00pm. Staff hours were even longer. They had to be on the counter ready to serve at least five minutes before the shop opened, although they were only paid from when trade commenced. Some mornings they had to be earlier to carry out tasks such as cleaning the brasses, and, after the store closed, they were expected to stay behind to clean and tidy up. Stocktaking was another chore which took place during hours when the shop was closed. None of this qualified as paid 'overtime', it was just part of the job.

Clearly, rates of pay changed considerably over time. How much individual employees received also depended on a variety of other factors: the type of job and work done; experience; length of service; and whether they were male or female. Apprentices were given annual rises of about two shillings a week, for example, but, according to Mr. Pyke, 'only subject to satisfactory conduct'. In the earlier years travellers received commission on their sales. In later years, although men continued to receive regular weekly wages, women, even those employed full-time, were paid an hourly rate so that their take-home pay varied from week to week. All this makes it difficult to generalise about levels of pay. On the whole it is likely that pay became less attractive relative to other occupations over time since shop workers were poorly organised and profit margins were gradually eroded over the century. Since T. D. Smiths did not recognise trade unions which were, in the words of F. B. Smith, for 'those who did not do their job properly', they did not pay the rates recommended by the unions in the later years, but wages were always above those stipulated by the Whitley Council set up after the 1914-18 war to provide minimum guidelines. Although somewhat less than the Co-op paid, staff appeared content with their pay.

The fact that Smiths was a family business seemed to generate a 'friendly,

TYPICAL WAGES, 1905–1955			
Year	Apprentice	Experienced Counter Hand	Senior/Charge Counter Hand
1905	6s	£1 8s – £1 15s	£2 15s
1925	8s	£3 3s – £3 18s	£4 8s
1935	7s 10d	£2 18s – £3 8s	£3 18s
1945	10s	£3 0s – £3 15s	£4 8s
1955	£2 1s 10d	£7	£10
from Staff Wages Book, Lancaster City Library			

Figure 5: *Typical wages, 1905–1955*

Plate 12: *Staff outing to Lever Brothers' factory at Port Sunlight on the Wirral to celebrate the firm's 75th anniversary in 1933. Mr and Mrs F. B. Smith are in the centre of the front row, with Mr and Mrs E. G. Smith to their right. Herbert Pyke is front right.*

Plate 13: *T. D. Smith's staff cricket team in around 1937. Back row (left to right): Mr Pilkington (non-employee, umpire), Charles Hillard, George MacGuire, George Elland, Dick Wilson, Ken Eason. Front row: Eric Butterworth, Eric Rushton, Herbert Pyke, Robert Beetham, Bill Robinson, Jim Redmayne, unknown. (Photo loaned by Jim Redmayne.)*

family atmosphere' which was reflected in long service of many of its employees and in the professions of loyalty and gifts presented by the staff to members of the family on their coming of age, marriage, or obtaining of public office. When E. G. Smith married in 1895 all the staff were entertained to dinner at his house where they presented him with a marble clock. Just over thirty years later, in 1925, F. B. Smith was given a clock and an oak barometer as his wedding present and on his elevation to the local bench in 1943 he received a silver salver and illuminated address from his staff.[11] When close members of the family died the shop shut for the day and employees attended the funeral. Although it was 'not done' for employees to invite the boss to their formal occasions, Mr and Mrs Bradley recall that F. B. crept into the church unobtrusively during their wedding ceremony.

The firm was also active in promoting activities for its staff. Annual dinners were regular features from an early date and culminated in a grand centenary dinner and dance in Ashton Hall in 1958. Regular treats and excursions were also arranged, the firm taking its workers to Knott End for the day in July 1911, for example, laying on food and entertainment at Preesall House.[12] For much of the century outings often had a vocational purpose, taking in visits to Hartleys or Stork Margarine. To celebrate 75 years of business in 1933 there was a trip to Lever Brothers at Port Sunlight, while for the centenary celebrations there was a visit to Rowntree's Cocoa factory at York. By the 1950s, however, staff were given the choice of where they wanted to go and most trips were to Blackpool, occasionally to Southport or, on one occasion, to Barnard Castle. Other activities were organised by the workers themselves. For a number of years after 1933 a cricket team played in the Wednesday league where, quipped James Redmayne, it was the 'strongest team in the league' but, explained Herbert Pyke, only because it 'propped up the table'.

The firm's concern for its employees'

material welfare is also well documented. In 1948 Francis Brian initiated a profit-sharing scheme and five years later a non-contributory pension scheme. This, he remarked at the centenary dinner,

costs a lot of money, but if it has added to the security of the staff and to their faith in the future, it has been ample reward.[13]

Proceeds from the profits were distributed at an annual general meeting or social at which F. B. and other branch managers gave reports of the year's trade.

The personal atmosphere generated within the company owed much to the involvement of family in the daily management of the shop. F. B. Smith always called his staff by their christian names but not on the shop floor, believing that familiarity in front of customers was not compatible with the firm's high-class image. Staff on the other hand referred to their employer as either Mr. Edward or Mr. Brian. Relations were, of course, not always smooth. E. G. Smith was often seen as a fiercesome character, pompous and autocratic, and even stern to look at. It was said that he could sometimes be quite rude and there can be little doubt that working for him was quite strict and regimental. His son, however, who was a director of the company from 1924, was, according to his staff's recollections, the complete opposite of his father. He had a very gentle nature, a great trust in people and appears to have been a reasonable man who was anxious to listen to advice from his employees. James Redmayne, for example, recalls that F. B. Smith heeded staff warnings that charging for deliveries was unpopular with customers. It was he who urged his senior staff to continue the business after his retirement, even loaning them some of the money they needed to establish themselves. Even he, however, was known to become very cross when under pressure. Mr. Seddon remembers one such incident:

I had been left to do a window display whilst F. B. went out. I really did not know what to do. I suddenly thought of filling the window full of Heinz products.

Of course, when F. B. returned he wanted to know – in a harsh manner – how much I had been paid for doing the display and why Heinz had not contacted him. I had to explain
. . .

Even so, he added, 'his bark was worse than his bite'. Another incident, recalled by Ian Smith, occurred during the Second World War when a woman came into the shop and wanted a box of matches, at that time a scarce commodity. F. B. had some with red tips but the lady wanted blue ones. During a time of severe shortage when supplies were difficult to obtain, he was not amused, but this was one of the very rare occasions on which he lost his temper with a customer.

Although the family remained personally involved in the day to day management of the shop, however, this did not preclude them from extensive involvement in the wider affairs of the district with both Edward Gorrill and Francis Brian also going on to achieve prominence as national leaders of their trade's organisation. Other members of the family achieved considerable success in different fields and contributed to a wide range of social activities in the town. As we shall now see, the Smiths were far more than simply provincial grocers.

Notes

1. Interview with James Redmayne, 15 March 1990.
2. Census Enumerators' Schedules, 1871; Trade directories as Chapter 2, reference 5.
3. Census Enumerators' Schedules, 1881.
4. Lancaster City Library, Staff Wages Books, 1904-66, MS 8056–8059; *Lancaster Guardian*, 21 March 1958.
5. Women are almost invariably listed as 'general shopkeepers' in the trade directories for late nineteenth-century Lancaster.
6. Interview with Annie Pyke, 14 February 1990.
7. F. B. Smith, 'How we operate on a thirty mile radius', *Grocery*, June 1937.
8. See chapter 5 for details.
9. *Lancaster Guardian*, 23 March 1907.
10. *Lancaster Guardian*, 21 March 1958.
11. Press cuttings in the family scrapbook.
12. *Lancaster Guardian*, 8 July 1911.
13. *Lancaster Guardian*, 21 March 1958.

5

Family and public life

AS the initial discussion of T. D.'s family background showed, the complex nature of family connections, an acquaintance with the hill farming community and strong Methodist associations were important assets that T. D. must have drawn upon in his establishment of a sound and secure business, particularly in his decision to set up a delivery service in the remote fell areas to the east.[1] As the firm became successful and established a sound reputation, this situation of dependence was reversed, with T. D.'s family being able to offer positive support to family and chapel. The Smiths' increasing importance was also evident in the public involvement of several of its members in the local community and political life of the town, culminating in the appointment of E. G. Smith as Mayor in 1928, and in his and F. B. Smith's prominence as presidents of the grocery trades' national organisation.

Above all, however, it is the family's continuing involvement with, and dependence on, the business that is its chief characteristic. Family support was crucial from the outset. T. D.'s sister, Jane, was his housekeeper for the first three and a half years until he married in 1862 when his new bride, Mary Gorrill, proved a valuable assistant. Living above the shop in Penny Street for over eight years, Mary was naturally drawn into her husband's career and became 'a great help in all matters pertaining to home, social, and business life.'

With an increasing family and a growing turnover, T. D. naturally looked to involve his children to assist him and to ensure the long-term survival of the business. On leaving school, each of his sons worked initially in the shop. It should be stressed, however, that no obligation was placed upon any of them to follow in his footsteps. T. D. and his wife determined rather to provide them with the 'highest education' they could afford and to let them determine their own career. 'We conceived it our duty', wrote T. D. in his memoirs, 'to give each boy and girl good all-round training and then for them, after seeing what class of subjects they made best out with, to let them choose and specialise onwards'. He was astute enough to realise the mistakes made in many family concerns when offspring were obliged to carry on a business for which they had neither aptitude or interest.

It was his second son, Edward Gorrill Smith, who showed most interest and much promise. Joining the firm in his teens in 1882, he became a junior partner in 1892 and joint partner in 1901 when he took over active management of the firm allowing his father, whose health was failing badly by this time, to retire to a new home at Moor Platt, Caton. Charles Hermon Smith, the fifth and youngest son, was also brought into the business, becoming the assistant manager, also in 1901, and junior partner four years later. The succession was continued when Francis Brian, son of Edward and his first wife, Lilian, entered the business in 1915, and took over as director in 1924.

These members of the family were expected to work their way up to positions of responsibility by undertaking a period of practical training like the rest of the staff.

Plate 14: *The Smiths and their sons in about 1890. Back row (left to right): Francis John (Frank), John, Edward. Seated: Thomas Davidson, Charles Hermon (kneeling), Mary Gorrill, Thomas (De) Davidson junior.*

Charles, for example, was required to gain experience of all the different areas of the business before becoming assistant manager: working in the cellars and warehouse, packing, travelling, dispatching, weighing up, stocktaking, cashiering, balancing books, branch shop work, and, of course, tea tasting. Like other apprentices, the sons were also sent to other firms to get a broader view of business practices. Charles was sent to Armitage's of Nottingham, for example, as well as to Harrogate, and Francis Brian gained experience at Harrod's in London and E. H. Booth's of Preston. As his son Ian recalls, 'there were no privileges for family members'. The only other member of the family who was directly involved for any period, however, was T. D.'s first daughter, Eva, who undertook the laborious and thankless task of book-keeper and cashier. Eva was the exception, however, and the other three daughters were not involved, a reflection of the widespread antipathy towards women working in trade at that time.

T. D., however, ensured that even those immediate members of his family not directly involved in the business shared in its success and stood to gain financially from its activities after his death. To this end he converted it into a private limited company in 1905, with £8,000 of preference shares divided equally amongst his eight surviving offspring, Edward Gorrill and Charles becoming joint directors and sharing the ordinary shares between them. In this way T. D. passed his wealth on and gave his daughters some capital and security, guaranteeing the continuation of their now comfortable existence.

Those who did not enter the business generally made good use of their education.

Joseph Smith (1775–1836)
m. Mary Glover (1799)

John Smith (1803–1882)   9 other children
m. Margaret Davidson (1838)

Thomas Davidson Smith (1838–1906)   4 other children
m. Mary Gorrill (1862)

Edward Gorrill Smith   John   Mary   Francis   Clara   Margaret   Thomas   Eleanor   Charles
(1867–1948)   1864–1926 1868–1950 1870–1919 1872–1944 1874–1951   De   1879–1972 1880–1941
m. Lilian Sharp   1875–1906

Francis Brian Smith (1898–1966)   Enid Mary Smith
m. Kathleen Parkinson   (d.1933)

Ian   Joesph   Felicity

Figure 6: *Simplified family tree*

For sons this had generally involved private tuition at home or at one of the local private academies, followed by a spell at Lancaster Royal Grammar School. The eldest son John then went on to study at Edinburgh and other universities, rising to become Professor of Surgery at Manchester. Thomas, the fourth son, also excelled academically, obtaining first-class honours at Cambridge and London, but died tragically young in 1905 after a short but promising career in teaching. Only the third son, Frank, proved to be a problem, expressing a desire to enter farming, much to his parents' disapproval. After various difficulties with his higher education to do with discipline and commitment, 'it was deemed wisest and best for him to follow the bent of his wishes'. After a year at Stubb Hall, Halton with his cousins, the Towers family, he emigrated to South Africa to stay with other relations, the Baynes family, where he pursued a successful career in farming.

T. D.'s daughters attended various private local academies including Miss Fisher's in Dalton Square, Miss Prestons and Mrs. Wordsell's, King Street and Miss Partson's of Regent Street before being sent to Arnside or Southport to complete their education. The problem T. D. faced then was a common one amongst the late-19th-century middle classes since none of these daughters was successful in the competition to find a suitable match. Whenever possible their parents sought to equip them 'to earn their living . . . or at least be employed in something more than home duties'. Eva initially helped out in the business and Nellie, the youngest daughter, successfully attended university at Cambridge and Dublin. Clarrie and Bessie remained at home to assist their mother but occupied their time with many useful and philanthropic activities, taking Sunday school and sewing classes, for example, and later becoming involved in many charity committees, following their mother's example by getting involved in nursing and serving on the committee of the Lancaster and District Nursing Society.

As well as financing the family's education, the business also provided the funds to house them comfortably. The cramped living accommodation in Penny Street had been far from ideal, T. D. complaining bitterly in his memoirs about the actions of a neighbour who extended his premises and cut off the light from most of his windows. Early in the 1870s they moved out to 3 The Vineyards, a terrace on the main road at Greaves just south of Lancaster, and then, in 1875, to 'Hermon House' (now Victoria House) on the corner of Regent Street and Lindow Square, a residence specially designed for them by the distinguished local architects, Paley and Austin, but adapted by T. D. since the cost was beyond his pocket. On taking over the business Edward lived for some time at 19 Thornfield on Ashton Road, but the family eventually spent most of their lives until 1944 at 'The Bungalow' on the prestigious Haverbreaks estate.

Despite their town base and business interests, the family did not lose touch with their rural origins. On his father's death in 1882 T. D. bought the family farm at Mealbank and spent over £1,000 improving it before renting it out to a tenant. E. G. Smith kept up this interest in agricultural affairs, helping to revive the Lancaster Agricultural Society after the First World War, bringing about the merger of local allotment societies into the district Horticultural Society to which he gave frequent lectures, and promoting shows in the district as far afield as Bentham. He, too, spent money on improving the Mealbank property before disposing of it in the 1920s. The Gamblesholme estate was only sold after his death in 1948.

The family also retained strong links with their early Methodism which linked them not just with the farming community but with an urban social network which incorporated many others from similar social and business backgrounds. T. D. was described as 'an ardent adherent'. He and his brother, William Glover Smith, who

Plage 15: *A family group around 1918. Back row (left to right): Clarrie, Francis Brian, Eva, Charles, Eleanor, Bessie. Middle row: Edward Gorrill, Lilian (E. G.'s wife), Mary Gorrill (Mrs T. D. Smith), Irene (wife of John), John. Seated on ground: Enid (sister of F. B.); baby Isabel. Seated child: Francis*

Plate 16: *E. G. Smith as president of 'The Federation of Grocers' Associations of the United Kingdom', pictured with the Association's parliamentary committee outside their new offices, 1932–33.*

owned a drapery business in Lancaster and lived next door in Regent Street for many years, were members of a close-knit middle-class religious community which was centred on the Wesleyan Methodist Chapel in Sulyard Street and included many prominent retailers, including Joseph Bell, with whom T. D. had spent time as an apprentice. Initially a Sunday school teacher at the age of twenty one, T. D. was later elected in 1869 to the superintendency for an eight-year period. Subsequently he was auditor of the school finances, a trustee of the Sulyard chapel and several other Wesleyan chapels, and, after 1891, a circuit steward, while his brother William was also circuit steward and choir master.[2] His daughters all became Sunday School teachers, as did Edward who also became superintendent in 1903 and president of the Lancaster and

District Sunday School Union in 1903 and 1911. He and his wife Lilian were also later actively involved in Greaves Methodist Chapel.[3] The family, therefore, were figures of some consequence in the local religious community. E. G. Smith retained links with his family's rural Methodism right up to his death, bequeathing £1,000 in his will 'to the governors of Pooley's schol at Wray with Botton . . . trustees for the time being of Wray Unsectarian Day School, to be applied . . . for the foundation of scholarship as a memorial to the testator's father, the late Thomas Davidson Smith'.

Although religious life represented the limit of T. D.'s public participation this was not true of his son and grandson. E. G. Smith became a borough magistrate in 1913 and a county magistrate in 1930, only retiring on his 75th birthday in 1943. An ardent Liberal, he was co-opted as a

43

Plate 17: *Mary Gorrill Smith. This portrait, along with that of T. D. Smith (right), hung in the shop's main office.*

Plate 18: *T. D. Smith in his later years*

member of the town council in 1916 for Park Ward, which he sat for unopposed until 1929 when he was elevated to Alderman. He served on and was chairman of many council committees including those for health, parks and housing and was particularly associated with the Watch Committee, which he also chaired. The pinnacle of his public career was in 1928-29 when he held the office of Mayor. In addition to this he was a Port Commissioner from 1917, governor of the two grammar schools, president of various horticultural societies, a member of the golf and rowing clubs, chairman of the cricket club, and head of the Federation of the Sports Union. He and his wife were also instrumental in founding the Lancaster

Lads' Club, the League of Help and the Y. M. C. A. which they supported by holding garden parties and other fund-raising activities at their house.[4] F. B. Smith was to continue this public role, though on a smaller scale. In 1943 he, too, was appointed a borough magistrate and he sat briefly as town councillor for the safe Conservative Queens Ward between 1954 and 1957.[5]

It was the involvement of the Smiths in retailing organisations however, that made them and the firm nationally renowned. The pace of retail change in the late-19th century encouraged the formation of trade associations designed to protect and fight for members' interests, both locally and nationally, by seeking agreements on pricing policy, for example, and by influencing the activities of local authorities and

Parliament. T. D. and E. G. Smith were both instrumental in forming the Lancaster Grocers' and Provision Merchants' Association in 1897 and held the office of president on several occasions, as did F. B. Smith in his day. But it was Edward who took this further, through his involvement with the National Federation of Grocers' Associations, a body established in 1891 to protect trade interests by linking together local associations throughout the country. After holding various committee posts in the 1920s, including chairman of the sports committee, he was elected President in 1932-3. This involved him in extensive public engagements such as attending annual conferences of local associations and the meetings of the Empire Marketing Board, lobbying parliament, especially for a change in the way Co-operative societies were taxed, making public speeches and entertaining foreign trade representatives. With his father, F. B. Smith edited a magazine called *Grocery* but he also became a prominent member of the National Federation in his own right, sitting on its Parliamentary Committee for twenty one years before following in his father's footsteps and becoming president of the organisation in 1951-2.[6]

By this time, however, the outlook for private grocers was less good. Although his inaugural speech to the federation blamed the continuation of government restrictions on trade for the plight of the grocery trade, there were more fundamental changes beginning to emerge in retailing which were to undermine the patterns of trade of men like the Smiths and with this, the financial security, public prominence and influence which they enjoyed.

Notes

1. Much of the following information and the unattributed quotes were obtained from undated press cuttings in the family album and from T. D.'s autobiography.
2. *Lancaster Guardian,* 8 September 1906; 29 April 1911.
3. *Lancaster Guardian,* 22 September 1928; 13 August 1948.
4. *Ibid.;* see also *The Grocer,* 19 October 1912; *Lancaster Guardian,* 17 November 1928 & 18 January 1930.
5. *Lancaster Guardian,* 14 May 1954; 20 May 1966.
6. *The Grocer,* 24 June 1933; *Lancaster Guardian,* 29 June, 1951.

Epilogue

IN 1958 a celebratory dinner was held in Lancaster Town Hall to commemorate the firm's centenary. The occasion was attended by some eighty employees, their families and friends. Among those making speeches and proposing toasts was J. E. Bell, whose family firm also dated back into the mid-19th century. 'I firmly believe . . .', he said, 'there is a place for the private trader in the commercial world'. F. B. Smith's speech, however, was more

Plate 19: *The Penny Street stores just prior to closure in 1961 (Albert Gillham collection).*

cautious. Regarding the future he was

> . . . making no promises to anyone but would endeavour to ensure that the interests of the staff would be safeguarded should anything happen to the firm.[1]

He had good reason to be cautious. Smiths' retail business had survived for as long as it had because it had been able to adapt to changing economic conditions without having to sacrifice the essential emphasis on quality and service upon which its reputation rested. In this it had been helped by the enterprise and personal involvement of its owners, the commitment and skill of its staff, the relatively slow expansion of price cutting and self service, and by improvements in technology and transport which had improved its efficiency rather than undermined its security. The business's roots, strengths and loyalties were also all essentially personal and regional, and the family had never sought to jeopardise what it held dear by further geographical expansion or dramatic change. But by the 1950s the pace of retail change was quickening. Rather than seeing a restoration of the profit margins of the early decades of the century which had allowed the maintenance of personal service, the end of rationing witnessed a quickening transformation in retailing methods and growing price competition, a process assisted by the outlawing of resale price maintenance whereby shops had only been able to sell goods at prices laid down by the manufacturers. The development of supermarkets, an American innovation, caused F. B. Smith particular concern since they were anathema to everything he believed in. Unlike E. H. Booths who, John Booth

46

recalls, reluctantly, but ultimately very successfully, embraced the new methods of retailing, Smiths remained wedded to traditional labour-intensive service. Unfortunately, increasingly price-conscious, mobile customers placed less value on this, and saw less need for deliveries.

With hindsight, then, it is clear that the firm's future was indeed very uncertain by the time of the centenary dinner. Only three of the branch shops then remained – Moorlands, Skerton and West Road – and their takings were low and dropping. They were to close in April 1959, April 1960 and October 1960 respectively. Gross turnover was also dropping steadily, from over £3,000 per week in 1957 to less than £2,400 by 1960.[2] On 23rd. September 1960 F. B. Smith announced that he was to retire due to failing health. Like T. D. before him he had allowed his children to make their own career decisions, the result being that there was no one to carry on the business. His sons Ian and Joe were beginning successful careers elsewhere and were ultimately to become professors of Chemical Engineering and Urology respectively, while his daughter Felicity had also moved from the district, pursuing a career in teaching before marrying. Although he continued to be associated with the shops at Grange, Arnside and Settle, with no one in the family to succeed him, F. B. Smith decided to sell the firm's central Lancaster premises to Greenwoods, the hosiery and outfitting specialists, who subsequently passed much of it on the Co-op, a move which F. B., who like his father and grandfather had fought the movement all his life, had sought to avoid at all costs.[3]

The traditions of the firm, however, lived on in Lancaster for another twenty years when some of the staff including Herbert Pyke, Tommy Seddon, Norman Bradley and the firm's accountant, Bill Edmondson, took up F. B.'s suggestion and offer of help to open new premises in Dalton Square. These opened in 1961, trading, with the family's blessing, as T. D. Smiths (Lancaster) Ltd.[4] Although initially continuing the rural delivery service the new owners concluded that this was unprofitable and were forced to abandon it in 1966. With the retirement of Mr. Pyke in 1981 after half a century with the firm, and the absence of anyone willing to buy the business as a going concern, the history of T. D. Smiths finally came to an end.[5] The firm's famous trade sign, a large green teapot which had hung over the entrance of the shop, was donated to Lancaster City Museum. A chapter in retail history had drawn to a close.

Notes

1. *Lancaster Guardian*, 21 March 1958; 27 June 1958.
2. Lancaster City Library, Account Books, 1957–61, MS 8063.
3. *Lancaster Guardian*, 23 September 1960. Most of the site is now (1991) occupied by Wilko's supermarket.
4. *Lancaster Guardian*, 27 January 1961.
5. *Lancaster Guardian*, 14 November 1980; 6 March 1981.

Occasional Papers from the Centre for North-West Regional Studies

Working-Class Barrow and Lancaster, 1890–1930	E. Roberts	£2.95
Flowering Plants and Ferns of Cumbria	G. Halliday	£2.95
Early Lancaster Friends	M. Mullett	£2.95
Traditional Houses of the Fylde	R. Watson/M. McClintock	£2.95
North-West Theses and Dissertations, 1950–78	U. Lawler	£6.00
Lancaster: The Evolution of its Townscape to 1800	S. Penney	£2.95
Richard Marsden and the Preston Chartists, 1837–48	J. King	£2.95
The Grand Theatre, Lancaster	A. Betjemann	£2.95
Popular Leisure and the Music Hall in 19th-century Bolton	R. Poole	£2.95
Industrial Archaeology of the Lune Valley	J. Price	£2.95
Roman North-West England	D. Shotter	£2.95
The Diary of William Fisher of Barrow, 1811–59	W. Rollinson/B. Harrison	£2.95
Rural Life in South-West Lancashire, 1840–1914	A. Mutch	£3.95
Grand Fashionable Nights: Kendal Theatre, 1575–1985	M. Eddershaw	£3.95
The Roman Fort and Town of Lancaster	D. Shotter/A. White	£4.95
Windermere in the nineteenth century	O. M. Westall	£4.95

Each of these titles may be ordered by post from:

C.N.W.R.S.,
Fylde College,
University of Lancaster,
Bailrigg, Lancaster

Books will be despatched post free to UK addresses.
Please make cheques payable to 'The University of Lancaster'.
Titles are also available from all good booksellers within the region.